The Golden Years of Flying – As We Remember

FRONTIER AIRLINES 1946 - 1986

The Golden Years
OF FLYING

As We Remember

FRONTIER AIRLINES 1946 - 1986

CAPTAIN TEX SEARLE

Aviation Supplies & Academics, Inc.
Newcastle, Washington

The Golden Years of Flying — As We Remember
Frontier Airlines 1946 – 1986
by Captain Tex Searle

Aviation Supplies & Academics, Inc.
7005 132nd Place SE
Newcastle, Washington 98059-3153
Email: asa@asa2fly.com
Internet: www.asa2fly.com

Illustrations and photos are used by permission. The author and ASA would like to thank
those who have contributed art and historic photographs for this publication. *Cover
photography*: Front cover top photo by Ted W. Miley; front cover bottom photo, courtesy
Stephen Gustafson Collection (aviationphotographs.net). Back cover photo provided
courtesy Jake Lamkins. *Inside photography*: pages vi and vii, courtesy Jake Lamkins, and
Stephen Gustafson Frontier Photo Collection; page 84, courtesy Stephen Gustafson; page
85; Frontier Airlines; page 152, courtesy Hans Melin; page 165, courtesy Bob Polanecky;
painting on page 9 by Richard R. Broome (used by permission). All other photos are
owned by the author.

Printed in United States of America
2012 2011 2010 2009 2008   9 8 7 6 5 4 3 2 1

ASA-GYF
ISBN 1-56027-708-4
      978-1-56027-708-8

Library of Congress Cataloging-in-Publication Data:
Searle, Tex.
   The golden years of flying—as we remember Frontier Airlines, 1946-1986 : DC-3 pilots
share their tales of a remarkable era of flight / by Tex Searle.—2nd ed.

      p. cm.
   ISBN-13: 978-1-56027-708-8 (pbk.)

   ISBN-10: 1-56027-708-4 (pbk.)

   1. Air pilots—United States—Biography. 2. Frontier Airlines—History. 3. Airlines—
West (U.S.)—History. I. Title.

   TL539.S36 2008
   623.16092'279—dc22

   [B]
                              2008043278

Contents

Acknowledgments

I especially thank Captain Jack Schade for his many contributions of true chronological accounts and comical tales. For his suggestions on the book and for the wonderful memories of the distant past we shared in the front office of a DC-3. Times and airplanes change, but as Captain Schade points out, flying a DC-3 was just about the best thing that could happen to a man. These memories of flying the Grand Ol' Lady will always be with us.

Many thanks to Captain Billy Walker for his assistance and detective work in locating many of the captains who have scattered around the good ol' USA. To all the captains and esteemed friends who contributed valuable stories and without whose enthusiastic encouragement this book would still be in the initial stages of hangar talk.

The author also gratefully acknowledges that many others provided valuable material and assistance to bring back those yesteryears.

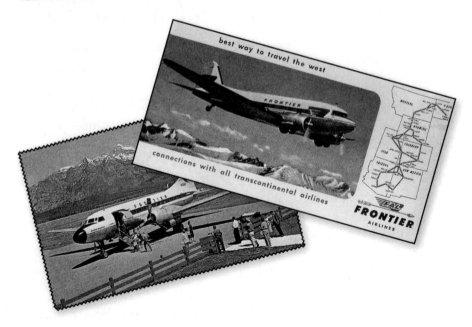

Preface

This book captures the lifetime legacy of flying the Rocky Mountain empire with Frontier Airlines and their highly specialized professional pilots. They devoted their lives to achieve for Frontier Airlines, and themselves, the best safety record in the history of civil aviation. This record was based upon the most stringent measure of the number of takeoffs and landings while flying extreme conditions. Frontier Airlines—not to be confused with the start-up company currently using the Frontier name—flew from 1946 into 1986. They flew safely and confidently from coast to coast, throughout Canada, and into Mexico. In her early history, crews handflew the old DC-3s over the high Rocky Mountains in and out of black holes to small airports hidden in deep mountain valleys to achieve this remarkable and enviable record. As Frontier Captain Billy Walker pointed out, "When the book was closed on the Frontier story, a large number of proud employees left a remarkable legacy for historians to ponder over."

The book touches upon the early history of aviation beginning with the first scheduled passenger flights and early transcontinental mail flights that developed into today's large airlines. It also invites you into the cockpit for a lighter dimension of aviation. You will surely enjoy the camaraderie of the crews, the high jinks and shared jokes they pulled on one another. Share the experience of flying through Tornado Alley without radar and of flying resolutely in canyons of moist, sodden clouds while lightning displays a mushroom of highlighted pageantry throughout the heavens.

Along with their stories I encouraged the pilots to write what enticed them into aviation. Some of these interests go back into the 1920s and '30s. I found that pilots shared a common goal of wanting to fly airplanes from the early days of their youth. Many have expressed that no one is interested in reading an old pilot's story. Having cajoled, threatened, and sulked to get this material—I'll let the reader be the judge of that.

Author's note about this new printing: The original novel was published 10 years ago by the author and this will be a third printing. Of those airline captains contributing these stories, nine have flown west. This was my goal; to save these Golden Years experiences before they too flew west.

1

Looking Back

In my twilight years I find that I am spending more time sitting in my favorite lounge chair on the patio watching the grass grow. But it is autumn now; the leaves are falling, the grass is not growing, and my attention is turned elsewhere. The sky is clear and I watch the undulating contrails of fast-flying jets, controlled by computers and automatic pilots, as they speed to predetermined destinations. The smoky sky makes a spectacular sunset and as stars begin to appear, I see the contrails fade, replaced by the flashing lights of aircraft proceeding in many directions to satisfy the requirements of a mobile society.

On some evenings, when a gentle rainshower has dispelled the smog and the skies have cleared, I see the reflected lights from satellites as they race across the heavens high above the blinking lights of transport aircraft. I wonder if they are manned or unmanned. Are they friends or foes? Are they from this world or another planet just checking to see if we are behaving properly; or do they have some other more somber motive? Against this backdrop I fondly acknowledge that my life has been consumed with the transportation of persons and things, and with flying aircraft of many shapes and characteristics.

As I reminisce back to those early years, it seems incredible, like a wistful dream. Did it really happen? They say that in a man's lifetime, he has to grasp the big opportunity when it presents itself. I was fortunate that a large part of my flying career involved the DC-3 (Douglas commercial number three) while she was still the mainstay for many airlines. They are the years I remember best, and it is because of the DC-3. Many pilots over the years have expressed their affection for the Grand Ol' Lady; it's almost as if she had a soul. When asked if they would do it over again, the consensus seemed to be you give me back fifty years and I'd spring at the opportunity. This says a lot and confirms the crews' affirmation: We were very close. The camaraderie is something you have to experience. The close association of Frontier Airlines DC-3 crews is not easy to explain, but it was there, and like the sound of the old recips, those memorable times from a prior era will always be etched in memory.

Over the years in my association with many of the old recip (piston engine driving a propeller) pilots, I became enraptured with the early flying experiences of these former seat-of-the-pants aviators who are such a grand part of aviation history, some whose careers began long before WWII. They flew many types of aircraft powered by the recips. They flew the old Jennys and Curtiss Pushers. They flew the big recips in WWII that powered bombers and famous fighters in the air wars over Europe and the Pacific. In a manner reminiscent of knights of old, they did battle one on one. A time in history that will never happen again. Many were highly decorated. Many were in the twilight of their careers when the jet age began to replace the recips. Yet, these prominent old pilots whose privilege it was to have flown the DC-3, without fail still speak of her with gentle affection and closeness that only they can understand. She returned their affection by giving the crews a feeling of camaraderie among themselves. The sands of time will never dim this memory. No other airplane has been endowed with such widespread feelings of devotion and remembrances by her crews.

In its early history, Frontier Airlines was unique in that it was the only airline expressly serving the Rocky Mountain empire. The name Frontier Airlines was appropriate in that it opened up a vast area never before served by scheduled airline service. Flying into the heart of the Rockies with little or no navigation aids, and weather that changed hourly, Frontier pilots mastered the art of mountain flying while serving small communities that lay in deep valleys with dirt and graveled landing strips that left no room for error. After landing, only the left engine was shut down for the purpose of convenience and saving time. MPX (mail, passengers, and express) were quickly exchanged, and after the loaded cargo and passengers were safely secured, the doors were closed and the left engine restarted. Climbing into the thin air to squeeze through high mountain passes, the

DC-3s would disappear like specks in the sky, continuing on to other scheduled rendezvous.

It seems to be true that when a man reaches his senior years, he can remember events of the distant past better than he can remember what happened yesterday. I can vividly recall lying on my dad's large stacks of hay as a youth, waiting for one of the old tri-motors to appear in the sky or to see the beautiful Western Air Express Douglas M-2 biplane on its run between Los Angeles and Salt Lake City. I remember the time a DH-4 biplane was forced down at the old Sand Hill strip in Delta, Utah. I skipped school and ran four miles to see this marvel that defied the laws of gravity, only to have it take off in a cloud of dust as I breathlessly watched from a distance. At the age of 12 I had the opportunity to approach and touch my first DC-3.

I remember a Barnstormer giving rides at the Sand Hill strip and going into debt to take my first airplane ride in a Travel Air 6000. I remember how small everything looked, how slow we seemed to travel over familiar landmarks, how noisy it was, the feeling of awe I cherished. I had found my lifelong dream.

At the age of 15 my prayers were answered. Carter and Woodhouse, a flying team, were at the old strip to give flying instructions in a Taylor Craft. I sold a steer, and with a craving lust I headed for the strip and struck a deal. After two blissful hours of cross-controlling and steering a roller coaster ride through the heavens while striving to hold straight and level flight, the deal quickly collapsed when my mother discovered one of her progeny had sold his four-legged asset and was living his dream. Once again I was back on the haystack.

2

First Scheduled Airline Service

My thoughts drift back to the time when, if an airplane was heard overhead, people would stop whatever they were doing to watch this wonder in the sky with great respect. In 1958, while seated in the luxurious cabin of a Connie in St. Petersburg, Florida, I observed the ground crew as they scurried about the Super G Constellation preparing it for the next leg. I remembered that the first regularly scheduled passenger flight had originated right there in St. Petersburg. At 10:00 a.m. on January 1, 1914, crowds thronged the waterfront to watch as Tony Jannus applied power to his 75-horsepower Benoist flying boat. Beside him sat a passenger who had paid five dollars. The small craft lifted off from the waters of St. Petersburg, Florida on schedule, and eighteen miles and twenty-three minutes later it touched down offshore from Tampa to complete its inaugural run as the world's first regularly scheduled passenger airline.[1] This service started just ten years and fifteen days after Orville and Wilbur's first powered flight. A few months later, after hauling over 1,200 passengers, the tourist trade began to decline and the first scheduled carrier had to shut down in the spring of 1914.

With this humble beginning, plans were already in motion to use aircraft for the future transportation of goods. Airline companies were formed that consisted of one-plane operations to those with several aircraft. In the twenties, Henry Ford acquired controlling interest in the manufacture of the famous Ford Tri-motor. Stinson came on line with its own Stinson Tri-motor. The Boeing Aircraft Company designed and built the Boeing Tri-motor, and then in 1933 it produced the world's first modern passenger plane, the Boeing 247. In the early thirties Donald Douglas, founder of the Douglas Aircraft Company, headed up an elite team of engineers that designed and constructed the

DC-1, then the updated DC-2 made its appearance. From the DC-2 evolved the world's most prominent airliner, the famous DC-3. The DC-3, which first flew in 1935, allowed many airlines to offer safe and dependable service. America was becoming air-minded, and now they had an aircraft to match their aspiring enterprises. By 1939, the DC-3 was carrying ninety-five percent of the world's airline business.

In the late twenties and early thirties, major airlines were under control of large aviation coalitions who were each prepared to wage stormy corporate wars to fulfill their visions of expanding their own companies into dominance. From these turbulent times emerged the "Big Four," directed by strong-willed chief executives.

With the forced departure of United Airlines president Phil Johnson in 1934 because of alleged collusion between the U.S. Post Office and the Big Four, W.A. (Pat) Patterson was elevated to the presidency of United at the age of thirty-four. Patterson, a financial expert and former bank executive, was not afraid to bump heads with postal officials.

WWI ace Eddie Rickenbacker brought Eastern Airlines into prominence. He had once served as a chauffeur for General Billy Mitchell, and Mitchell had made it possible for him to learn to fly. Captain Eddie was this country's highest-scoring ace in WWI with a total of twenty-six aircraft gunned out of the skies.

Texas born Jack Frye, a stunt flier and flight instructor, helped establish Standard Airlines. Standard was acquired by Pop Hanshue's Western Air Express which merged into TAT (Transcontinental Air Transport) that later became TWA (Trans World Airlines), sometimes referred to as the Lindbergh Line. Jack Frye came aboard and was soon elevated to vice-president. Shortly after that he was made president at the age of thirty. His search for a better passenger plane was instrumental in the development of the DC-1 and the DC-2.

Originally, the DC-3 was conceived of as a luxury sleeper by the solicitations of innovator C.R. Smith of American Airlines, who encouraged the development of the DST (Douglas Sleeper Transport) as a replacement for his airline's dated twin-engine Curtiss-built Condors, a smaller, enclosed-cabin biplane that accommodated seven convertible berths for sleeping. The larger aggrandized DST was designed for seven upper and seven lower berths with a cabin forward. Searching for more payload, it was soon discovered that by removing the berths twenty-one passengers could be comfortably seated; with this modification the ever-revered DC-3 evolved. Under the leadership of C.R. Smith, American Airlines was the foremost air carrier for two decades in terms of passenger miles flown.

During the wrangling and competitive posturing in progress among the Big Four and others—coupled with their altercations with Postmaster General Walter Folger Brown who wielded a heavy hand to implement his version of the transcontinental airways map—emerged Juan Trippe, a Yale graduate. A pilot himself, Trippe walked, talked, and dreamed of building an airline empire. He knew his way around Washington, and he groomed influential friends who would provide support and backing when he needed it. His keen instincts made him aware of the potential of international flights, and with his talent for obtaining landing rights in foreign countries, he was setting a course for his airline empire.

He built his fledgling carrier into what became known as Pan American World Airways. Under Trippe's leadership, Pan Am's dazzling flying boats with luxury interiors became a pacesetter for years to come. He dressed his crews in dark blue uniforms and gave the first pilot the title of "The Captain." The white hat with a visor was worn by crews flying the Pacific, and the blue visored hat was worn by crews flying the Atlantic. The copilot became the first officer, a tradition that was followed by other airlines. At the completion of a trip, no personnel exited the aircraft until the captain had deplaned.

Crews in Hawaii were always lodged at the Royal Hawaiian, and the captains had their own separate quarters in the building as well as an area on Waikiki Beach that was sectioned off for their personal use. When turning in at night, Pan Am crews left their shoes outside the door for a nightly polish.

Trippe brought the world to the doorstep of the United States. There will never be another time when romance is so closely associated with aviation. The large China Clipper flying boats, named after the swift and magnificent Clipper sailing vessels that plied the China tea trade in the mid-nineteenth century, took you to faraway, romantic places, such as Key West, Havana, Nassau, the West Indies, Panama, and Puerto Rico. They flew the vast reaches of the Pacific and Atlantic oceans.

In those bygone years everyone dressed for the occasion; it was all uptown. Male passengers always wore a suit or a sports outfit (mostly white) with a necktie. It was easier to identify female passengers since most of them wore attractive dresses making them look every bit the lady. Today's passenger terminals have taken on the mantle of busy bus stations, and ticket agents are threatened occasionally for mistakenly addressing a female patron as "Sir."

As a youth, I dreamed of those things. It's not that way now, but I still think about it. As with many other airlines, the modern advent of deregulation was a contributing factor in the demise of Pan American World Airways.

3

First Mail Flights

DH-4 crossing the Rockies. —*courtesy artist Richard R. Broome*

As far back as 1911, there were infrequent and unofficial attempts at flying the U.S. mail. But with inferior equipment, few experienced pilots, and the inexperience of managing an operation of such magnitude, these efforts met with little success.

When the Allies began taking the offensive against Germany, signaling the end of WWI, a surplus of both experienced pilots and sturdy, more powerful aircraft became available. With the element of derring-do and despite proven hazards, a bold plan was set in motion by the Post Office to implement reliable mail service beginning May 15, 1918, using Army pilots flying the Curtiss JN-4H.

Three months later, civilian pilots were hired by the Post Office to replace Army pilots. They flew the Standard JR-1B that had a 150 horsepower Hispano-Suiza engine that was soon replaced by the surplus

DH-4 with a Liberty 400-hp engine. Two years later the mail service had expanded from coast-to-coast.[2] The pages of recorded history are filled with accounts of unwavering, dedicated pilots who confirmed their willingness to uphold the tradition "the mail must go through."

Pilots were fired for refusing to fly in potentially dangerous weather. One pilot was fired by the headstrong Second Assistant Postmaster General Otto Praeger for his sensible assessment in refusing to fly in fog that cut visibility to less than fence posts; other pilots were fired for similar conditions.[3] Even today, with modern instrument landing systems, scheduled flights don't operate into airfields with that kind of visibility. Without instruments or navigational radios, the only plausible course for the pioneer mail pilot was to keep visual contact with terra firma.

Praeger pushed once too hard, and the pilots called for a strike. It was quickly settled when Praeger backed off and let the pilots judge the weather, with the exception that a field manager could challenge the pilot's judgment. But with the challenge, the field manager had to go aloft in the aircraft with the pilot to determine whose judgment best summarized the existing weather conditions.[4] With only enough room in the single cockpit for the pilot, there wasn't much of a problem after that resolve.

Night Flying

Before Jack Knight flew his first-section, experimental night flight from North Platte to Omaha, the mail was being carried by Post Office DH-4s only during daylight hours. As darkness descended, the mail was loaded on trains to continue the journey across the continent. Financial institutions and many business enterprises encouraged the postal officials to fly the mail around the clock. The Post Office was acutely aware that for continued mail service to be feasible, night operations were a necessity. On the first experimental transcontinental night flight, the heroic Jack Knight, after flying his leg from North Platte, Nebraska to Omaha continued on to Chicago in weather that had kept his relief pilot from arriving at Omaha. Knight saved the first experimental night flight from failure.

Knowing the mail could be carried around the clock, the government made money available for improvements on the transcontinental mail route. Plans were made to update DH-4s to make them more suitable for night transportation of the mail.

Rotating beacons would mark the airway over the entire route. Emergency landing fields were to be constructed. The beacon lighting was completed in the mid-1920s and proved its worth with a much improved safety record. The turn and bank gyro, used by pilots to keep their aircraft upright in poor visibility, become a reality. More flights got through, and the number of on-time arrivals of scheduled flights was vastly increased.

The aural-null compass for aerial navigation was made available in 1924, and airway routes were laid out like an invisible path in the sky to guide the way by radio compass. This modern marvel allowed pilots to rely on the radio compass to reach their destination while flying blind on a black night, or obscured in clouds. In the twilight years of government mail transportation by air, these old airmail pilots could only marvel at the dawn of invisible electronic pathways through the sky.

The Kelly bill—entitled the Air Mail Act—was passed by Congress and signed by President Coolidge in February 1925. This bill permitted the Post Office Service to advertise for bids on the feeder routes that delivered mail to the transcontinental route. The passage of this bill permitted private contractors to carry the mail in their own planes. The Air Mail Service would be phased out over a year's period and on July 30, 1927 the last mail was carried by pilots under the direction of the Post Office Department. During the last year of operations pilots had flown 17,500,000 letters over 2,500,000 miles. About 40 percent of this had been flown in darkness and the overall rate of schedules met was 94 percent.[5]

The pioneer mail pilots who flew from 1918 through 1927 were a special breed for whom flying the airplane and the mail to their destination was a challenge not to be turned down. This was accomplished in aircraft without proper instrumentation for weather flying, and with insufficient engine power for the high mountainous terrain they were called upon to fly. Thirty-two pilots and nine mechanics had been killed in the line of duty. Three hundred planes had crashed; however, most of them had been salvaged and some flew again.[6] They paved the way for today's fast and safe airline service.

First Contract Mail Flights

The first CAM (Civil Air Mail) flight, designated route 5 by a private carrier in the west, was flown by Varney Airlines April 6, 1926. The pilot climbed into a small underpowered biplane called the Swallow as it revved up to make the first CAM flight from Pasco, Washington to Elko, Nevada with a stop at Boise, Idaho. Twenty-five-hundred spectators had amassed at the dusty field to wish him well. After a scheduled stop at Boise, the flight arrived safely in Elko where the mail was transferred to the transcontinental trunk route still flown by the Post Office.[7]

After struggling through lean years, Varney Airlines, with better mail rates and good management, eventually started to show a profit. It was later sold to United Aircraft and Transport Corporation, a holding company that ultimately would be called United Airlines. Many of today's surviving airlines along with American, Trans World, and Delta, either merged into or bought out established companies.

Tailspin through the Clouds

Fred Kelly was hired December 1, 1925 as the first pilot for Western Air Express before its forced merger with Transcontinental Air Transport, instigated by Postmaster General Walter Folger Brown to reinforce the transcontinental route structure. The surviving routes of Western Air Express not enveloped in the merger were eventually reorganized and flown by the renamed Western Airlines. In 1946, while serving as Vice-President of Operations for Western Airlines, Captain Kelly spoke to a group of new-hire copilots, among which was Jack Schade who later served as a senior captain for Frontier Airlines. Captain Schade was kind enough to pass on Captain Kelly's account of early day instrument flying describing the pilot's efforts to deliver the mail.

> **Captain Kelly:** *In this time period, Western was flying CAM route 4 between Los Angeles and its Salt Lake City terminus where it connected with the Transcontinental Mail Route. Flying beneath a low, solid overcast, the pilots flying the early mail route had to deal with all kinds of adverse weather conditions and eventually worked out an understanding with the Union Pacific Railroad locomotive engineers to always be alert for signals asking the train to stop. The pilot would land and discuss with train crews the current weather conditions from their boarding terminus to its present position. Usually this would determine whether the flight continued on or remained on the ground waiting for improved weather conditions.*

A fine-tuning of weather reporting came about when one pilot made friends with a railroad maintenance supervisor who lived near the head of the pass leading down into the Los Angeles area. If the Western pilots found the mountains obscured in weather, they would descend and rev their engine at the head of the pass. The supervisor regularly checked the narrow confines of the pass to observe the weather conditions, and if his prognosis was in accord with favorable reports he had received from the train crews, he hurried to the head of the pass waving a green lighted lantern. The pilots seeing this signal knew the cloud base and visibility were acceptable for their bizarre flight maneuver in the Los Angeles basin.

The pilots climbed to a terrain-clearing altitude and then checked the time. Flying a predetermined compass heading over the cloud-obscured mountains until the fixed time ran out, they would then ease the nose up and kick in full rudder forcing the aircraft into a spin through the clouds. After spinning out the base of the clouds they recovered normal flight—clear of the mountains they continued on their route of flight.

If the cloud base was low, the railroad supervisor signaled this information by waving a red lighted lantern; pilots then landed to wait out the weather. So much is taken for granted today where flying and weather are concerned, that we fail to pay tribute to the pioneer pilots who were determined to advance the science of aviation from a devil-may-care exhibition to what it is today.

The Lighted Airway

Captain Schade tells of an early period in his career when he was flying with Challenger Airlines (one of three predecessors of Frontier Airlines). He was issued information pertaining to the transcontinental beacon lit airway that was part of Challenger's route. In this time period the airlines were using the all weather, Adcock Low Frequency Range Navigation method with Morse code oral signal of the letters "A" and "N" to keep them centered on the airway. Navigating by radio was still in its infancy with its bulky weight and unreliable vacuum tubes.

Captain Schade: *A United Airlines flight navigating the airways from Salt Lake City to Denver had suffered a complete radio failure. The flight was in danger of being trapped as daylight was fading and the weather was rapidly deteriorating over the planned route ahead and closing in from behind. Unable to navigate or communicate without a radio, the pilot pulled out the old airway beacon chart and followed the guide lines. They safely flew beneath the weather from beacon to beacon over the old transcontinental beacon lit airway used by airmail pilots in the 1920s.*

The elevation of each beacon above sea level was established, and pilots learned the magnetic heading from beacon to beacon. From the list of beacons furnished to the DC-3 pilots of Challenger Airlines, each beacon could be identified by a Morse code letter that flashed its own identifying signal from below the large flashing, airway beacon. It was mandatory that Challenger pilots know each beacon's code and elevation. Being aware of the upcoming beacon and flying just above its elevation provided a backup for a pilot when everything else had failed.

It was decided to use the Morse code identifier so the pilot could readily recognize each beacon site and identify his present position at all times on the lit airway. The identifier code, mounted below the large, flashing beacon, was a special light that flashed its Morse code letter to inbound aircraft. Knowing the distance between beacons, the pilot could also check his speed over the ground by using his timepiece. The old beacon lit airway was a welcome sight as its friendly flash greeted the pilots flying into the dawn of an new electronic era. Much of it was still in operation long after WWII.

From the ever dangerous Allegheny Mountains, known as "The Hell Stretch," across the open plains to the towering regions of the Rocky Mountains with their thin air and craggy peaks, and continuing westward beyond the Sierra Nevada Mountain Range to California, the original airway beacons were a godsend to the lonely pilot feeling his way along the desolate route. Recognizing the flash in the far reaches of a black night was like a greeting from an old friend, and he eagerly flew his craft towards this most important landmark.

AIR MAIL PILOTS

FROM THE FILES OF CAPTAIN JACK SCHADE

Fourteen below zero,
Mercury droppin' fast
Just now I heard a mail plane,
As it went a-splutterin' past.

And, I think, as I'm sittin' here
My feet agin the fire,
I'm wonderin' how cold it is
A half a mile up high.

And I'm wonderin' what in thunder
Kind of "guts" that feller has,
That was drivin' that dumb airplane
That just went a-zippin' past.

It's two a.m. along this river,
He was makin' one hundred flat,
As he steered that blame critter
Up the valley of the platte.

Then, I hear another a-comin'
A-diggin' for the East.
A-sliddin' o'er this valley,
Like the blame thing was greased.

This country now is covered
With about ten feet of snow,
And every night the mercury
Drops to twenty-two below.

But, them two guys a-riddin'
Workin' for Uncle Sam,
Surely don't know how cold it is,
Less they don't give a damn.

And I keep a-thinkin' of 'em,
Are they just a pair o' nuts?
Or, are they a couple of "he-men"
With a belly full o' "guts"?

—AUTHOR UNKNOWN

4

Back When

Captain Floyd Ririe was the patriarch of senior pilots on Challenger/ Frontier Airlines, and served as chief pilot for Challenger Airlines when it began operations in 1947. He learned to fly in the 1920s and has done it all, from the early Curtiss Pushers to the Jenny (WWI trainer). He transported medium and heavy bombers as well as fighters in WWII. They say he was born with a joystick in his hands and a smile on his face. Crows feet extend outward from the squint in Ririe's eyes caused by many hours straining to find his way among seas of clouds and the bright rays of the sun in an open cockpit biplane, and from searching lonely night skies for a friendly beacon to show him the way. He is one of the few true pioneer pilots left in Utah, and he credits his longevity as a pilot to the guardian angel who had been riding on his shoulder at the time he suffered a serious bicycle accident at the age of eleven. This was the first time he had worn a surplus WWI helmet purchased some months before the accident, and it saved his life when his head crashed onto the pavement.

I served as one of Captain Ririe's many copilots, and knowing I was interested in the early history of aviation, he related fascinating accounts of his personal experiences to me. He described the years when forced landings were as common as apple pie. Once while piloting an open cockpit biplane whose engine had sputtered and quit, Captain Ririe made a successful forced landing in a pasture in Carbon County, Utah. While troubleshooting the engine, he discovered the carburetor had become loose on its mount. He borrowed some barbed wire from a nearby fence, wired the carburetor back in place and cinched it down with a pair of sidecuts that were part of the required repair kit carried for just such an emergency. Ririe then took off from the pasture and continued on his merry way to Salt Lake City.

The *Los Angeles Times* recounts an incident when Ririe was flying a newly-constructed International plane with a 90-horsepower engine fresh out of the shop. As he approached the landing field with an inexperienced student, ground personnel ran to the runway and pointed at the little International's landing carriage. Ririe discontinued the approach and pulled up. He checked the wheel on the right side; it checked normal. Checking the left side he discovered the wheel was not in place. Further investigation revealed the locking cap on the left axle had worked itself loose, allowing the axle and mounted wheel to slide free from the underneath fuselage support. As the spreader bar with the attached wheel swung to and fro beneath the fuselage, the fuselage gear supports on the right side held it from slipping free of the aircraft.

Ririe yelled through the prop wash directing his student who occupied the rear cockpit to remove all the safety wire from the turnbuckle connections that gave added safety protection to the various components in the cockpit. Ririe did the same in the forward cockpit. Without a parachute he climbed out on the left wing, stretching out with his elbow hooked over the leading edge of the wing to keep from being blown off by the slipstream. Two thousand feet of air separated him from terra firma, and a green student was doing the flying. With his free hand he reached down and gripped the wheel assembly and managed to pull it upright. He tried several times before he was able to reattach the axle and wheel to the under-fuselage support. Then wrapped the safety wire around the axle in place of the missing locking cap. Ririe had feeble hopes it would keep the wheel assembly from slipping off again, but he crawled back into the cockpit and flew the little International back to the airport. As he softly touched down on the dirt strip, he held the left wheel off the strip until the low airspeed let it down. After a short roll the wheel and axle again came loose. The aircraft did a half ground loop causing only a couple of scratches to the underside of the wing tip. Besides making a newsworthy item for the *Los Angeles Times*, Ririe made the cover of a 1920's *Mechanics Illustrated* sitting on the spreader bar attaching the wheel to the axle.

Continuing with the phasing out of the Air Mail Service, the Post Office had put its entire operation of the transcontinental air route between New York and San Francisco up for bids to competing private enterprises. National Air Transport was awarded the New York to Chicago segment and Boeing Air Transport was awarded the Chicago to San Francisco segment. In 1929 Ririe was flying the trimotor as copilot on the night run between Salt Lake City and Oakland, California.

Captain Ririe was among the first of Utah pilots to be awarded the Air Transport Certificate and has many memories of flying for Boeing Air Transport. When the trimotors first came into use, copilots also served as cabin attendants and had the assignment of calming nervous passengers by keeping them updated on the flying conditions. One time, while picking their way through the Sierra Nevada Mountains at night, and trying to stay below the murky weather, they flew at 8,500 feet in order to follow the highway through the canyon. A passenger came forward and said, "There's a lady going nuts back there." As copilot, Ririe went back to determine her problem. She pointed to the large altimeter on the forward bulkhead and in an excited voice yelled, "You can't fly over the Sierras at less than 10,000 feet." When Ririe explained they were not flying over the mountains but through them, she calmed down.

Through mergers, stock buyouts, and some court action, Boeing Air Transport became United Aircraft and Transport Corporation and gained control of the continuous New York to San Francisco transcontinental air route. From this growth emerged United Airlines.

Impasse

There was one concern while flying the Boeing Trimotor with her three engines. If it became necessary to shut one engine down from loss of oil pressure, you would be unable to feather the propeller. The marvelous invention that would streamline the propeller into the wind, halting its rotation, was still in the planning stages. Besides the increased drag the propeller caused, the wind pressure against the propeller kept it rotating. In this impasse, the propeller now drove the engine instead of the engine driving the propeller. If you were forced to shut an engine down for lack of oil pressure, some quick decisions would need to be made. The internal friction of the engine would cause overheating, and you would soon have an engine freeze up, or possibly a fire. To avoid this, it was necessary to land as soon as possible in the nearest pasture or on a road.

The Indispensable Bottle

The early bi-wing Boeing Trimotor was built during the 1920s. Her rugged dependability and ability to land in short fields while hauling twelve or more passengers in wicker seats made her popular with early air-minded travelers. With a cruising speed of only 110 miles per hour, the two crewmembers spent considerable time in the cockpit droning away the hours flying to their destination. There was no blue room (rest room) in the aircraft so they kept a bottle in the cockpit to take care of their immediate needs. It was necessary for the crewmember using the bottle to stand and lean against the cockpit door, which opened inward to the cockpit from the cabin, to ensure privacy.

Captain Ririe told of a friend who upgraded from the Trimotor to the newer Boeing 247 that entered service in 1933. It was the first of a new generation of passenger aircraft having retractable landing gear, higher airspeed than the old Boeing Trimotors, and room for ten passengers. The one big concern: the bottle remained an indispensable item for the crew's flight kit since the blue room was still inaccessible.

The upgrade created a problem for my friend on his first trip in the new Boeing 247. Flying with a captain who kept his eyes aimed forward and his mouth shut, the friend, on short notice with little to do, felt an urgency to use the bottle. As per the usual custom, he stood and leaned against the cockpit door. Everything was under control until the door popped open. Then all hell broke loose! In one sudden instant, he lost his self-respect. After falling partway into the cabin, he quickly picked himself up. But, to his humiliation, everything else had splattered into the passenger cabin; where it landed he never asked.

Utterly mortified, he quickly closed the door and meekly strapped himself in his seat. The captain was still glaring stoically ahead, only now his face looked more like a Japanese sumo wrestler. After that curtain call, my friend made no further announcements in the cabin for the continuation of the trip. And never again did he forget that the cockpit door opened outward to the passenger cabin in the new Boeing 247.

Ririe's Grand Finale: *Eventually, Boeing Air Transport lost three of its Boeing Trimotors from accidents. Business was slow and with layoffs I was out of work. In the throes of the great depression—steady work was hard to come by—I worked at various flying jobs and barnstormed around the country to scratch out a living.*

For sport I recall equipping an ancient Curtiss Pusher with skis. In the late fall we would shoot geese from the Pusher, and then land to retrieve them. In the winter we shot coyotes.

One year when Cedar City, Utah was having its annual rodeo, I was selected to give them a little excitement. Flying an old J6-5 Eaglerock, I stuffed a pair of coveralls full of rags and put it in the forward cockpit. After doing loops and rolls, I rolled the Eaglerock over on its back and held it there until the dummy fell out. I let the biplane fall into a tailspin, but when I tried to recover, I discovered the biplane wouldn't respond to the normal spin recovery procedures. I was beginning to wonder which dummy was going to hit the ground first. I tried everything in the book to recover and was beginning to feel the day had arrived that I was going to "buy the farm," when a voice said, "Push the stabilizer ahead." So I pushed the stabilizer ahead, cracked the throttle, and pulled up. It took about ten minutes of flying around the countryside to regain my composure enough to get the Eaglerock back on the ground safely. I was describing to a friend what happened, and he said, "Yah, I saw you, and if you ever try that again, you SOB, I'll kill you." The little man on my shoulder had saved me again.

With the advent of WWII, Ririe served as a major in the Army Air Corps. The fighter he particularly enjoyed flying was the famous P-38, but his most enjoyable pleasures came from flying B-24 and B-25 bombers to Australia.

Captain Ririe served as the first chief pilot for the newly-established Challenger Airlines in 1947. Many of the pilots who flew the mountain empire with Challenger/Frontier were hired by Captain Ririe. From the memory files the following story was remembered.

Hand Prop

Captain E.P. Lietz (retired) was flying copilot for Captain Ririe when a starter broke down on the DC-3 at Rock Springs, Wyoming. With the station agent observing, Ririe hand-propped it like it was a J-3 Piper Cub. "Contact!" he shouted. E.P. switched the ignition on as Ririe swung the prop. The engine coughed, belched out a mushroom of blue smoke, started and then settled down into a deep throb. They taxied out, and continued the flight. In the annals of DC-3 memoirs, I have never read of anyone hand-propping a 1,200 hp Pratt & Whitney Double Wasp engine. It's hard to imagine something like that happening now. With archives that are overburdened with Federal aviation regulations, the FAA (Federal Aviation Administration) would have you hogtied and facing the guillotine before sunset.

Captain Ririe turned ninety-one on December 4, 1997. He said he had given up water-skiing at age eighty-six after injuring his shoulder while mowing the lawn. Captain Ririe had to retire from Frontier thirty-one years ago because of the mandatory age sixty requirement put into effect by the FAA. After living much of his life in the air, Ririe now spends his time tending his yard—occasionally looking up when a high-flying aircraft reminds him of a career full of memories. He dryly comments, "With today's reliable engines, automatic pilots, computers, and backup systems, could one ever know of a time when flying was really seat of the pants flying?"

A Tribute To Captain Floyd Ririe

Captain Eldon P. Lietz: *I have one comment concerning the event when Floyd Ririe hand-propped the DC-3 engine to start it. I don't think it's unreasonable to suppose that the DC-3 could be started this way, but I do not know many men who would be strong enough and have the proper* touch to start one this way. I vividly remember when I was very young my uncle took me to the Salt Lake City Airport. It was just a very large dirt field then without marked runways. A DH-4 biplane was being started. Although I am not an expert on the DH-4, I'd guess the engine was about 400 horsepower. About seven men stood in a line holding hands. The one just under the engine grabbed hold of the propeller blade, and then all seven of them pulled the prop through and it started. The DC-3 had a heck of a lot more horsepower than that (1,200-hp). It was all I could do, with my shoulder against the prop, to push the blade about two feet. Floyd took hold of the trailing edge of the blade with both hands, threw his right leg into the air and pulled down hard. The engine spun through three blades and started. It took a really strong man to do that.

I first met Floyd in 1938, who is just about the most man that I have ever encountered. Whenever anyone wants to talk about a real airplane pilot, Floyd is who they are talking about. I flew airplanes myself for 42 years and came in contact with many different pilots. Floyd was absolutely at the top of the heap.

Floyd was the most unusual man I have ever known. He was a Major based at the Long Beach Army Airfield when I joined the service. At that time I was a civilian pilot employed by the Army Transport Command awaiting my commission. I was very young, looked even younger than I was, and had only seen Floyd at Thompson's Air Service at Salt Lake City. I never flew with him then. I walked into Base Operations when Floyd was there. He immediately walked over, shook my hand, and wished me luck. A lot of guys would have never even recognized me. After the war Floyd hired me on the airline where he was Chief Pilot of Challenger. Floyd was and still is deserving of all of the credit and attention due a very fine and very capable man.

5

Early Day Weather Predictions

To the early pilots, weather was always a phenomenal patchwork of speculations to be reckoned with. Many pilots and passengers alike thought their own weather prognosis to be more predictable than the questionable reports they received from unschooled forecasters. Like farmers, some early pilots would gauge the weather by the moon. If the moon was encircled by a full halo, a storm was expected before another fortnight arrived. When the moon was in the form of a crescent and a powder horn could be hung on it, or if it could serve as an upright water dipper, then rain was not forecast for the near future.

A more reliable forecast was possible if Uncle Archie's lumbago or Aunt Wilma's rheumatism began to act up—a sure sign that unfavorable weather was lurking near. If these predictions all failed, they then referred to the *Farmer's Almanac*.

Some put their trust in the cricket, a very "scientific" method for determining the current temperature. Even though they couldn't afford a thermometer, many of the old-timers could tell the precise temperature on a warm night by listening to a cricket chirp: the higher the temperature, the faster the cricket chirped. They then added thirty-seven to the number of chirps per 15 seconds which would approximately equal the current temperature (close enough for government work).

A heads-up pilot used a more predictable form of forecasting by determining the cloud types and watching the barometer. Widely-scattered cumulus clouds and soft-blowing breezes, along with a steady barometer, were signs that fair weather would prevail. A falling barometer with the wind velocity increasing from out of the south or southwest and gray altocumulus clouds moving in from the north or northwest, were indications of an approaching storm.

When the clouds cleared and the barometer was rising steadily with light breezes, the old pilots would bundle up for the expected colder temperatures.

Sea-going crews on old sailing vessels would scan the horizon in the evening and early dawn to determine what the weather might be. Red clouds at night, sailor's delight—red clouds in the morning, sailors take warning. Many early pilots observed these same warnings.

The Wasatch Front, a beautiful range of the Rocky Mountains bordering Salt Lake City on the east, extends north and south for several hundred miles. Weather forecasters had a difficult time predicting the weather for this region. Active weather fronts moving inland off the Pacific Ocean continue from the northwest into Utah. As the systems approach the Wasatch Front, they occasionally build in intensity and may arrive earlier than predicted with more severity. Other times they lose intensity or their predicted movement over the surface is slowed. Early pilots used their own intuition as to what type of weather would be encountered near the Wasatch Mountains.

At times, snowfall was unpredictable. Affected by the temperature variations caused by the Great Salt Lake, now known as "lake effect," the lake temperature would affect the surface temperatures and also the humidity that would vary from the known conditions along the Wasatch. These environmental factors would sometimes cause a much greater snowfall than had been forecasted.

During winter months with snow on the ground, the cold air mass at the surface becomes trapped by the warm air aloft, commonly known as an inversion. This may last from the middle of December until the latter part of January unless a strong frontal system can break down the high-pressure area and clear the valleys of the cold damp moisture. Each day an inversion continues in the valleys, smog and fog increase and visibility decreases. In the evening hours, the dense vapor continues to increase and visibility continues to decrease—often to zero.

The Rocky Mountains have an assortment of complex weather patterns unique to the mountain regions served by Frontier. In early spring, aircraft approaching the old Stapleton Airfield at Denver which lies at the foot of the front range of the Rockies, were subjected to heavy turbulence from the prevailing westerlies whose high winds roared down the mountain slopes. Winds over eighty mph were not uncommon along the range, extending from Fort Collins to Colorado Springs, at times leaving extensive damage behind.

The roll cloud in its stationary position above the high peaks along the front range of the Rockies is a familiar sight in the late spring and early summer to those pilots who pay sharp attention to this phenomenon. The affliction of unwary pilots caught in this horizontal whirlwind is ingrained into their learning steps as they progress up the ladder of knowledge. Frontier crews were well-versed on avoiding these dangerous areas over the Rockies.

This variety in weather patterns is what pilots had to contend with in the early years. The coming of radio aids to guide planes to the runway in inclement weather was a welcome milestone. The airline crews who flew in the 1940s and '50s had to contend with higher weather minimums for landing due to inferior navigational aids. Many crews descending into the Salt Lake valley would have their approach clearance cancelled because of below landing minimums at the runway: an unpredictable fog had suddenly moved in. If the runways at Salt Lake City were closed because of insufficient visibility and Ogden and Provo were also down, the old DC-3 crews were left to stretch their dwindling fuel reserves to reach distant alternates. There are many stimulating accounts of crews who endured such marginal situations while drawing on all their expertise to make proper decisions.

The Black Hole

Before radar, every old-time pilot, through wisdom gained from experience, had his own fundamental principles on how to assault the weather. One old cliché that makes your hair stand on end cautions that when ambushed at night by a brigade of advancing nimbostratus that towers into cumulonimbus, discharging firepower every which way, you quickly withdraw from any further engagement. If disengagement was not possible, you charged into the vacated black hole caused by the recent lightning discharge before it had a chance to reload. Some of the old ferry crews during WWII practiced this procedure when ambushed by thunderstorms in the mid-Pacific, and through the years some even lived to tell about it.

Elk Mountain is a protrusion of rocks rising to 11,156 feet, higher than the old mailplanes such as the DH-4 could normally fly. If running late and striving to make up time, some pilots were tempted with flying the more menacing but more direct course from Laramie to Rawlins or Cherokee, Wyoming. This shortcut required them to fly over the higher elevations south of Elk Mountain instead of taking the longer, dog-legged route around its more manageable northern slopes.

In the early years of radio navigation, the old low-frequency airway range would dog-leg aircraft over the Medicine Bow radio fix north of Laramie before letting them proceed westbound, so they could avoid the higher terrain of the Medicine Bow Mountains and Elk Mountain. With airlines flying unpressurized equipment, this made it possible to fly safely at lower altitudes for passenger comfort and to circumnavigate the mountains safely while flying in inclement weather. There were still disasters awaiting the imprudent. Elk Mountain's high summit, obscured in clouds, is the graveyard of several aircraft that flew off course for undetermined causes. One appalling cartoon shows a large vulture perched on the peak from above the clouds waiting for his breakfast to arrive.

On October 6, 1955 United Airlines Flight 409, for suspect motives, was flying over twenty miles left of the airway while en route to Salt Lake City from Denver. The DC-4 crashed into the high peaks of the Medicine Bow Mountains killing all sixty-six aboard, including many members of the Mormon Tabernacle Choir.[8] It was the worst commercial air-travel disaster in U.S. history at that time. More passengers were killed in this one crash than the combined total of all mail pilots killed during the Post Office tenure from 1918 through 1927. Some pilots believe the captain of flight 409 was attempting the shortcut; they speculate he was flying the DC-4 at treetop level through the cloud-shrouded mountains.

6

The H-Marker

In the late forties and early fifties only ten percent of Frontier's routes operated over Federal airways. It became necessary for Frontier to install some type of reliable navigational facility in order to operate in inclement weather over its own routes so instrument approaches into the small airports it served throughout the Rocky Mountain west could be executed.

The radio beacon chosen was made available as surplus property and was called the H-marker. It was the same beacon used by the Army Air Corps in Europe during WWII. It operated in the 200–400 KC band, nondirectional type radio facility that tied into the ADF (Automatic Direction Finder) installed in the DC-3s. It transmitted a continuous homing signal from which the pilot could determine the aircraft position in relation to the H-marker. At one time there were over twenty markers operating over the system. Each beacon also had a three-letter identification call sign that was transmitted in Morse code every ten seconds. After cranking the coffee grinder (frequency tuner) to tune in the selected H-marker frequency on their route of flight, the pilots would know with assurance they had the proper H-marker selected by listening through the earphones for its three-letter Morse code identifier signal.

Frontier crews became very adept in using H-markers for instrument flying in and out of the most difficult airports, some lying in deep valleys obscured by clouds and surrounded by steep mountains with high elevations. Several airports, including Gunnison and Alamosa in Colorado, Flagstaff in Arizona, and Laramie and Kemmerer in Wyoming, had elevations well over 7,000 feet. Some airports were located on high plateaus.

Airports with high elevations required a longer takeoff run for the DC-3. If there were several inches of snow on the short runway, aircraft performance was reduced even more. Crews taxied to the very end of the runway before turning around. After lining up for takeoff they locked the tailwheel and set the brakes before calling for full power. It wasn't necessary to check the takeoff charts as they do in transport category aircraft. They didn't have any because the DC-3 was built before such things were thought of. Regardless, she couldn't have performed to the stiff requirements of these limitations.

Pushing the throttles to the stops (it was impossible to overboost the engines in the high, rarefied air) the crews waited for the oxygen-starved Pratts to rev up to what power was obtainable, and then they released the brakes. As the Grand Ol' Lady strained to gather speed down the runway, the crew watched and waited while the far end of the runway drew near. She sometimes teased a little, but always managed to obtain flying speed and lift off before reaching the end of the runway.

Flying unpressurized equipment, Frontier crews were unable to coax the DC-3 to fly over the higher precipitous terrain. They flew between mountain ranges and crossed from one valley to another flying through high turbulent passes. This often put them in the middle of tempestuous weather with heavy icing. They logged a notable amount of instrument time flying under the most complex wind and weather conditions.

With an H-marker installed on each end of a pass, they regularly flew unhindered through such passes as La Veta Pass in Colorado on instruments. La Veta Pass, with its heavy cloud cover, is flanked on one side by Mount Blanca rising to 14,390 feet, and on the other side by Spanish Peaks rising to 13,720 feet.

An article in *Frontier Magazine* by editor Captain Chick Stevens relates an incident that occurred at Chama, New Mexico shortly after Frontier had installed an H-marker there for a navigational fix designating the pass:

The pass is located about sixty-five miles east of Durango, Colorado. The Chama H-marker worked fine until one evening flight into Durango reported the homing device was inoperative. This condition continued every evening for two weeks before it was discovered that the individual who operated the electrical substation at Chama had been cutting off the power to the H-marker so the farmers could have additional electricity to run their milking machines.

In the winter prevailing westerlies and low-pressure storm fronts continually sweep across the Rockies. Frontier pilots became immune to the turbulent air and went about their business of hauling passengers and mail throughout the mountain empire. Frequent Frontier passengers thought a rocky ride in the DC-3s through the Rockies was a way of life. It is said that an air traffic controller once advised his cohorts not to request any ride reports from Frontier pilots: "For what a Frontier pilot would classify as just light turbulence is, in actuality, moderate or greater turbulence to the aviation community."

Frontier's Air Traffic Control

Three of our DC-3s would converge at Riverton, Wyoming from the major points of Billings to the north, Denver to the southeast, and Salt Lake City to the southwest. (Maybe this was the first of the hubs that are so popular these days.) If all three flights arrived the same time and weather was involved, we would act as our own traffic control. When the pilot at the lowest altitude would start his descent to the airport, he would report vacating the various altitudes. The following pilot would report leaving his assigned altitude to descend to the altitude just vacated, and so on until all flights were safely on the ground. This procedure was reversed at departure. As the lead take off DC-3 reported vacating an altitude on the climb out, the next in line would begin his climb to the vacated altitude and so on until they were high enough to break off and proceed to their various destinations. A great deal of time was saved in marginal weather using this method of keeping flights safely separated in the perimeter areas of the Riverton Wyoming Airport. This same procedure was also used at Farmington, New Mexico.

While on the ground, all three flights were refueled and cargo was transferred from one to the other for continued transport to final destinations. The crews met in the crew quarters to pass on the latest scuttlebutt. These were happy gatherings. When departure time grew near, the crews would board early to check the fuel load, do a walk-around, and complete the checklist on the aircraft they had been assigned to fly back to their home domiciles.

Before we had PA systems, when flying was down-to-earth, we would send penciled notes to the passengers in the cabin to pass on information about important landmarks we would be flying over, such as Jackson Hole, Wyoming, Grand Teton National Park, Yellowstone National Park, the Grand Canyon, Mesa Verde National Park, the Royal Gorge, and Black Canyon of the Gunnison National Monument; plus the many ski resorts and prominent mountain attractions too numerous to mention. We carried our share of prominent folks from the film industry as well as important politicians. No airline could compete with Frontier for the birds-eye view of grandeur panorama presented by our flight crews.

7

The Director of Flight Operations

Everett (Ev) Aden

Whether he was training or overseeing check flights, Chief Pilot Ev Aden of Monarch/Frontier demanded strict discipline from those involved. In the end it paid dividends to both the company and the pilots in having the best safety record ever in the airline industry. Frontier pilots knew they had been well trained to master the art of carrying MPX (mail, passengers, and express) throughout the Rocky Mountain empire.

Captain Aden was a precise disciplinarian and a perfectionist. He expected his pilots to know the capabilities of their aircraft to its limits. His crews had to know the names and memorize the heights of all the major peaks and passes that they flew over and through. He questioned the pilots on their knowledge of every canyon and the location of every landing strip. He made sure they were well-versed in the various weather patterns they could expect to encounter over the mountains.

In their early careers many crews had Captain Aden as an instructor or check pilot. Over and over he would hone them in the proper use of the manual loop for navigating when all else had failed. How well crews remember Aden giving a bearing he wanted intercepted which led to Denver radio station KOA, frequency 850 KHz. It was proper procedure for both pilots to listen to the three-letter Morse code identifier to positively make sure they had the correct H-marker tuned in. But the Denver station was a commercial broadcast station and rarely identified itself other than on the hour or half-hour. If a positive identification was not made on the station to the satisfaction of Captain Aden, crews might find themselves attempting to shoot an approach into North Platte, Nebraska from a wrong frequency that was mysteriously tuned in. Using the broadcast station kept the training flights outside the perimeters of the traffic flow into the Denver airport. (In later years it was not uncommon for training flights to travel several hundred miles to a less active airport to accomplish the required flight training.)

The pilots being checked could expect to receive a clearance to intercept a track to the Denver radio fix and were also requested to give a timed estimate of arrival. The pilot first located his present position in relation to the station, then determined the heading to fly to intercept the inbound bearing at ninety degrees. By operating the manual loop antenna, he determined the time-distance to the station by noting the time it took for the aural-null needle to show a ten-degree change in direction in relation to the station. All this had to be accomplished while holding the aircraft on a steady heading, and if the estimate to the station was less than 2 ½ minutes, it would be necessary to make a 270-degree turn away from the station before tracking inbound. During this procedure with Captain Aden, certain instruments would mysteriously begin to fail until the flight instruments were down to needle, ball, and airspeed.

Or an engine would unexpectedly fail. This caused the DC-3 to immediately yaw into the bad engine. A pilot's reaction would be to immediately apply the proper rudder application to remain established on a straight path. Constant awareness was stressed in training to use proper procedures to identify the failed engine. We still remember the prompting: "Right engine! Left engine! Which is it? The rudder pedal you push to your course identifies your good engine. I give you books and you eat the covers."

To properly identify which engine had failed may sound like a simple procedure, but throw in a few problems as mentioned and a negligent pilot may find himself behind the power curve trying to quick-start his brain. Captain Aden insisted that all Frontier crews be able to react to any unforeseen problem as though they were in cruise control and his pilots be drilled to the extent they would be at ease navigating by whatever radio or instruments were available.

History testifies that over the years a few last farewells were hastily expressed because of unplanned descents—some because the good engine was mistakenly shut down. A recent newspaper article related the distressful situation inflicted upon one crew hauling contract mail, departing from Boise, Idaho at night. Shortly after takeoff an engine became engulfed in flames. The ensuing investigation revealed the crew of the cargo airline had mistakenly shut down the remaining good engine, preventing them from making an emergency landing at the airport. There were no survivors. Frontier crews had none of that.

When the air work was completed, Captain Aden might give a clearance that called for the crews to shoot a circling approach to runway 12 at the old Stapleton airfield. After cranking the coffee grinders to 378-KC, they would positively identify the DEN radio fix by listening to its Morse code signal, da dit dit – dit – da dit. Using the manual-loop to navigate by and with the weather reported at minimums (sometimes lower), they could expect to lose an engine at anytime. While approaching the radio fix the gear would be lowered, and after the crew had made visual inspections out the side window to verify that the gear was down, the final check was called for. When Captain Aden called landing checklist completed, it was a cue for those who had experienced this before to recheck the green light that indicated the gear was down and locked. Knowing the gear warning horn could be mysteriously silenced, when they rechecked, more often than not they would discover a red warning light had replaced the green light. When Captain Aden was queried on this he sometimes answered innocently, "What do I know? I'm just a dumb copilot." The gear latch handle would be quietly latched down again and the landing gear handle returned to neutral. If anyone failed to catch the red glow of the gear-unlocked warning light, they were afraid to venture a guess as to what might happen to them on the debriefing. It was best not to forget.

Inbound over the radio fix and approaching minimums, the hood would sometimes be removed indicating they were clear of the clouds. If it wasn't removed, they pulled up, cleaned up the airplane, and did it all over again. As this was to be a circling approach to runway 12, the pilot's response had to be immediate. After station passage he banked the DC-3 right to a heading of 210 degrees, and then instantly banked left 90 degrees to the runway heading of 120 degrees. While doing all this, it was necessary to get the gear back down and locked as Captain Aden had failed an engine after the final check had been completed. To keep the DC-3 in the air while flying on a single engine, it was critical the drag be reduced by raising the gear and leaving it retracted until you were certain you had the runway made. Tensed for a go-around if the call should come that a cow had wandered onto the runway, crews were always happy to hear the welcome squeal of the runway. Pilots claimed they could always plan on a ten-pound weight loss during a proficiency check. But to quote the adage, "perspiration forestalls expiration," it all paid off when making a tight approach in the lonely confines of the Rocky Mountains.

Captain Aden was born in Rising City, Nebraska about fifty miles west of Omaha. Later the family moved to Wheatland, Wyoming to live on a ranch. The owner took young Ev up in a Piper Cub for his first ride, and it was then that Ev knew where his future lay. When old enough, Ev quit his job and entered the Wheatland Civilian Pilot Training Program set up by the government to train pilots for the growing Army and Navy aviation programs. Ev continued his education at the University of Wyoming, and later at Cheyenne, he got his commercial license and instructor rating; then, as Ev relates:

With war clouds hovering near, I joined the U.S. Navy as a flight officer. After my indoctrination I served as a primary flight instructor in Stearman biplanes. After a year of instructing I transferred to a flying boat squadron at Patuxent River, Maryland. I flew the big twin-engine PBM Mariners and the four-engine PB2Y Coronados to Bermuda, Puerto Rico, Trinidad and down the southern coast of South America to Natal, Brazil. This is where I got my non-directional navigation experience which proved most beneficial during the early Monarch/Frontier days. When the squadron closed, I transferred to Olathe, Kansas to fly the Navy R4Ds (DC-3). While there I took the CAA written and flight check for the ATP and DC-3 rating.

There was one unusual experience that I witnessed and will never forget. I had departed Amarillo, Texas on a beautiful clear night flying a Navy R4D to Phoenix, Arizona. As we passed over Tucumcari, New Mexico, the sky lit up so bright that we didn't need to use cockpit lights. I saw a white cloud rise well above our altitude of 10,000 feet and form a mushroom shape. I estimated we were about 150 to 200 miles from the cloud. I called every CAA ground station from our position to Winslow and received reports of shaking like an earthquake and a loud bang, but no one had a clue as to the cause. The next day, the paper said there was an unknown explosion at Alamogordo, New Mexico and no one was hurt.

Upon returning home, I told my wife I didn't know what we experienced but it certainly was not unknown and it was big. A few days later,

Hiroshima was bombed and I knew then I had seen the first test explosion of an atomic bomb.

Captain Aden joined Monarch in December of 1946, and accepted the chief pilot position four months later. When Monarch/Challenger/Arizona Airways merged in 1950, Captain Aden became the Director of Flight operations. He served 13-½ years in a supervisory capacity. With the rumor of jets on Frontier nearing fruition, Ev elected to return to line flying so that he could fly the B-727.

Throughout Frontier's system, Captain Aden became known as Captain Cheerio for his friendly greetings and sign-offs. Under his direction Frontier crews became known as the best airline mountain and H-marker pilots in the world. Other governments called upon his expertise to work with them on their flight programs. He was called to Iceland to establish the physical locations of H-markers for Flugfelag Island Airlines and the pilot training program. He was called to work with the Saskatchewan Government Airways in the proper usage of the H-marker and to work with them in setting up their training programs. Captain Aden received his Canadian Air Transport Rating, and is still a rated Canadian Air Transport pilot.

Captain Chick Stevens, editor of *Frontier Magazine*, wrote that the instrument checks Aden gave captains every six months were so tough that the pilots would think they were supermen if Aden told them they had done a good job. Many Frontier pilots received their Air Transport Rating through his program.

With all his contributions to safety, Captain Aden still found time to fly the lighted cross over Denver every Christmas Eve. The large, lighted cross was mounted on the belly of a DC-3. Captain Aden is listed in the Denver *Post*'s Gallery of Fame for having flown the lighted cross for thirteen consecutive years.

In 1981, Captain Aden piloted flight 74 from Guadalajara, Mexico into Denver, and parked the Boeing for the last time per the FAA requirement that airline pilots retire at age 60. For this last Frontier flight that Captain Cheerio would command, his first officer was Emily Howell Warner, the first female pilot of any regularly-scheduled U.S. airline.

8

Tidy Up the Cockpit and Bail Out

Captain E.P. Lietz, another Frontier captain, had that sparkling type of personality you enjoyed being around. If your mood was like a Monday morning wash, he would soon prevail upon you with his bank of stories. E.P. was a captain who could make life in a cockpit interesting. From E.P.'s own notes, here are a few of his experiences.

Captain Eldon P. Lietz: *I have told so many stories in my life that sometimes I have a hard time remembering. However, my procedure for two engines out would be to "Tidy up the cockpit and bail out." Ev Aden got a little upset with me when I came up with that during a checkride once. This was back in 1950 right after the merger when Bob Lambourne and myself were taking our final captain upgrade checks with Aden. Bob was already a captain but when Challenger and Monarch merged, Ev personally wanted to check each captain himself.*

I was on a localizer approach under the hood at Phoenix. I went down to minimums and Ev said, "You are not contact and you just lost all of your radio equipment. What are you going to do?" Now mind you, the way Ev had set this up, any place I could have gone to was below minimums. To compound the problem I had no radios to communicate with, or any navigation radios at all. There just was no way I could have gone anywhere flying by instruments. So I told him I would tidy up the cockpit and jump out. He blew up, yelled for a little while and then told me to land the airplane. When we were finished he said, "E.P., that was the worst checkride anyone has ever given me. But, I absolutely have to have a captain tomorrow morning and you are the only pilot available. I am going to have to pass you." He didn't make me feel very good.

In actual practice, if this had ever happened to me I would have just held my heading and continued to let down until I hit the ground. I can't think of anything else that could have been done.

Actually, this did happen to me once. I was the copilot on a C-46, and we were just coming over the range station in China. This was during WWII. The engineer went down into the belly of the airplane to tinker around with something and managed to short out the radio equipment with a screwdriver. We did not have any radio equipment. The ceiling was about six hundred feet. We were on top of a cloud layer and there were about six other airplanes ahead of us holding for clearance to start an approach.

The captain just got in line and followed them, keeping close track of the headings. He also kept track of the time elapsed between one airplane starting a descent and when the next one did. When the airplane ahead of us started down he timed it, and when time was up he dropped the gear and flaps, pulled off all of the power and down we went on that heading. We broke out at about 600 feet above the ground and finally found the airport and landed. Had we not been on top when all of this happened we would have been dead.

Not All Things That Happened Were Practical Jokes

A long time ago, perhaps around 1948, I remember flying copilot for Captain Charlie Weed in the DC-3. They used to pack the cargo hold just behind the crew with chickens bound for somewhere between Rock Springs and Billings, Montana. They smelled a lot. I remember one day Charlie looked back at the chickens and said, "You used to call me sweetheart. Now all you can say is cheap, cheap, cheap."

One day they loaded a large dog in the cargo bin. The poor thing got airsick, puked and made a mess all over. You talk about smell, that really did. We did not get paid extra for that.

In those days the copilot even had to do most of the cargo unloading. That brings back memories: I remember standing on the wing of a DC-3 at Rock Springs de-icing it with a kitchen mop and a big bucket of alcohol. We sometimes helped the stew sort all of the mail in the A compartment so the agent at the next station got the correct mail. And we did all that for the princely sum of two hundred dollars a month. At first, we didn't even get our expenses paid. Later they paid us seventeen cents an hour for meals and cab fare. It didn't hack it. Wonder why I stayed at that for two years. It gradually got better however.

I went to work for Challenger (predecessor to Frontier) in November 1947. Two days before Christmas 1947, they called me into the office and gave me fifty dollars. That was the first pay I had received. Got my wife a used vacuum cleaner for a Christmas present. I remember going into the head office one day and everyone working there was sitting on the floor. The company that supplied the fuel had cut us off and would accept nothing but cash. The office personnel sold all the furniture to get enough money to buy fuel.

Kids

I also remember flying with Woody Reynolds. He was a Challenger captain when he left to become Vice-President of Operations for Bonanza Airlines. He was just about the same size I am: short. We walked out to board the airplane and one of the passengers that was standing there went back into the terminal building and turned in his ticket. He said he was not going to fly anywhere with "those kids" doing the flying.

Mercy

And speaking of kids, it was tough enough trying to get enough mor aside for a flying lesson, but before WWII people thought you ho your rocker. There was no way a guy could earn a reasonable l' airplanes. When I started, I did it because I just loved to fl' were not paying their pilots enough to live on. When m' I was flying airplanes, she actually had someone comr counsel me. I was told that I was really wasting m' counselor knew aviators in California who were aviation career started out sort of strangely. I

42

against my flying airplanes, so I'd go to church on Sunday, walk in the front door, then out the back door, rush to the airport, take a lesson then dash back to slip in the church's back door in time for the service to end. My sister got upset with me one day and told mother what I was doing. "Mercy!"

One particular flying lesson I remember was at Thompson's Flying Service in Salt Lake City. I had to save my money for about three months before I could afford the price that it took to get a J-2 Cub up high enough to safely spin it. The instructor I drew that day was sort of a relaxed individual. After I kicked the J-2 into a spin, I was sitting there going around and around trying to hold down the last meal I had eaten, and he was eating a sandwich and singing "South of the border down Mexico way." I cotton pickin' near puked. He wound up as the commanding officer of an Air Transport Command Base in the upper Assam Valley when I was flying the Hump as a green Second Louie.

I Am Not Just Another Pretty Face

During the Boeing 727 days, I flew the last leg of a trip into Denver. As luck would have it I really greased on the landing. Pretty good if even I said so. When the passengers started to deplane, I opened the cockpit door and stood there watching. A lady stopped and said, "Captain, that was the most beautiful landing I have ever seen in my life." I replied, "Lady, I am not just another pretty face." She started laughing so hard that she almost fell down the airstairs.

Scrooge

Okay, here's another one. It was Christmas time, and I was flying a Boeing 737 through Omaha. My wife, Shirlee, had picked up a pair of deer antlers made out of cardboard she had found somewhere. Again full of the Christmas spirit. I took the antlers and put them on my The stewardess painted my nose red with her lipstick and voilá!

Rudolph the red-nosed reindeer was flying the airplane. Every time we stopped, passengers brought their little ones up to the cockpit and put them on my lap while they took pictures. We pulled into the ramp at Omaha and there was the current FAA Inspector assigned to Frontier. He was going to give me a checkride into Denver. Well, the whole thing just got unreasonable. Old Scrooge was really bent out of shape that I would do such a thing, and when we got back to Denver he wrote me up. I never really got into trouble over that. At least someone thought it was funny but the "fuzz" sure didn't. Other than the name Scrooge, I can't remember what his real name was, but he was a real blankety-blank.

We were trained to share duties with the other crewmembers, and help them become better pilots in any way we could. Old Scrooge even got upset over that. Riding with me on a Boeing 737, he gave me a hard time over duties that I assigned to the second officer that we normally did. Old Scrooge was bound and determined the second officer on a Boeing 737 was going to do nothing but sit there. Regardless of the FAA's attitude, this second officer later became an excellent captain.

Author's comment: If I knew I was to have an FAA Inspector aboard and occupying a seat in the cockpit, I would usually ask the flight attendant to load up a tray with all the goodies she could heap on, and serve it to our unwanted guest. This hedge usually worked, and his pursuits were diverted elsewhere. Isn't there an old proverb somewhere that implores one to "feed thy antagonist"?

Captain E.P. Lietz retired many years ago after a remarkable career of flying in the military and for Challenger/Frontier Airlines. He had the following to say about Frontier Airlines:

It was really a great airline. I have visited a lot with pilots of other airlines and I have come to the conclusion that I was fortunate getting to fly with Frontier. We had a more relaxed workplace, the pilots were much better than those on other airlines and a lot friendlier also. For me it was fun to go to work. I wouldn't have changed anything in my life if I had a chance to. I feel very fortunate to have worked in such a great environment doing something that I enjoyed very much and doing it with people who I enjoyed and I knew were superior pilots in every way.

E.P.'s flying goes back to when airplanes had strange-sounding names, and he has flown a variety of transports, plus some bombers that were converted into transports. As a command pilot in the military, his duties had him flying all over the world. Along the way he picked up the coveted Distinguished Flying Cross. Captain Lietz's logbooks add up to a total of over 34,000 hours accumulated while serving as a command pilot for the military, and a career of thirty-three years served with Challenger/Frontier Airlines.

Many airline pilots who began their career when the DC-3 was the mainstay, spent considerably more time in the cockpit compared with today's generation of pilots who are involved with duty rigs and monthly pay formulas. Many early Frontier captains logged over 30,000 hours during their military and airline careers. You won't see that anymore.

The passion for flying was so great in some pilots, that even though they were accomplished in other professions such as architecture, pre-med, pharmacy, and a captain who was also a lawyer, they followed their hearts and chose a flying career with Frontier.

9

Growth of an Airline

Monarch Airlines headquartered in Denver, Challenger Airlines headquartered in Salt Lake City, and Arizona Airways headquartered in Phoenix merged into a single airline in June of 1950, and the appropriate name Frontier Airlines was fostered. One year later they were operating from Montana throughout the Rocky Mountains to the Mexican border and had carried 138,000 passengers. Frontier now consisted of twenty-one DC-3s with 400 employees.

From the first flight of Monarch in 1946 into 1956, Frontier carried 1.5 million passengers, and the number of employees grew to seven hundred, of whom ninety-eight were pilots. Pressurized Convair 340 series aircraft came online in 1959. The fast and dependable Allison propjet-powered Convair 580, called the Mountain Master by her crews, made its appearance in 1964. In 1966, with the acquisition of Boeing 727 tri-jets, Frontier carried 1.6 million passengers in that year alone. With a fleet of thirty-seven DC-3s slowly being phased out, the last flight of the DC-3 for Frontier Airlines was flown in 1968 after serving faithfully for 22 years. Thirty years after the first flight, Frontier managed a fleet of fifty-two jetliners and propjets; they had hauled thirty-seven million passengers, and were projected to carry 3.7 million passengers in the year 1976.

Upgrading from the Convair 340 to the Allison Propjet 580 was a real pleasure; everyone loved to fly this sturdy aircraft with its excess power. When it came to landing at high-elevation airports, she was everyone's favorite. She was a twin-engine airliner with seats configured to haul fifty-three passengers which she did with ease. She was powered by two Allison jet engines geared to drive the largest four-bladed propellers I had ever seen (13 feet, 6 inches in diameter). Each water-injected engine was power rated at 4,000 horse power—

Allison Propjet 580

almost as much power in one engine as a B-17 had in all four engines. The Allison Propjet 580 and the high-elevation airports Frontier regularly served (some near 8,000 feet) were made for each other. We landed at higher elevations than where some aircraft cruised.

For a propeller driven plane, she was fast. You could push her up to 355 mph in a hurry, and she wouldn't even whimper. In sustained cruise, she was the fastest propeller driven twin ever in scheduled airline service.

How well I remember when the initial jets appeared on the scene and spectators ignored the DC-3 to admire this new, sleek, faster mode of travel.

Twenty-five years after the last DC-3 had been retired from Frontier, Captain Jack Schade and I had the opportunity to pilot a chartered DC-3 to Denver from Salt Lake City to pick up the mail. Following our arrival at the itinerant aircraft parking ramp in Denver, the Grand Ol' Lady graciously received an audience of viewers who surrounded the venerable DC-3 with cameras and their questions. I suppose what goes around comes around.

Returning to Salt Lake City in the predawn we followed the freeway west out of Rawlins, Wyoming flying at a low altitude. Just as they used to, and to our delight, truckers blinked their lights at us and we flashed our landing lights in return. This nostalgia-filled trip took us back to the time when flying was seat-of-the-pants stuff for the old Air Mail Service pilots.

In the early sixties with the phasing in of newer aircraft, the DC-3 would move on to begin a new life with other proprietors scattered around the world. Pilots have both cussed her and loved her, but she always did what was asked of her. She began life when wood and fabric were still the mainstay of the airliners. She was here when the jets first made their appearance and she still endures while many of them have passed on. Sixty-three years have passed since she made her first flight in 1935.

Several generations, from grandfather to son to grandson, have had the opportunity to stoke the fires in her big reciprocating engines. Now that we've moved into the 21st century, she is still flying and the crewmen who were around at the beginning may have passed into the blue horizon. When the Grand Ol' Lady makes her final flight into the blue horizon, and her soul glides in for a landing at the pearly gates, she'll hear the acclamation, "Well done."

Hi-Tech Navigation

It seems like only yesterday that I sat encased in a pressurized Boeing full of computers that I could program to literally do all the flying from takeoff to landing. I had auto-throttles that managed the power, and a coupled autopilot receiving information from unknown navigation facilities could direct my aircraft to anywhere in the world with little planning. With this hi-tech convenience I knew my location at any given moment; a far cry from the little Weems E-6B hand-operated computer we carried around in our shirt pockets in DC-3s.

When making an approach to an airport concealed in low clouds, the autopilot is coupled to the approach mode, and this marvel of latter-day wonders does all the work. With seemingly little effort it maneuvers the airplane down through the weather to the threshold of the runway more smoothly and more precisely than I can, and, if called upon it will even make the landing. As the aircraft approaches minimums to find the runway visibility obscured, and the decision is made to initiate a go-around, all that's necessary is to push the go-around switch on the thrust levers and the big jet spools up, pitches up and climbs for the safety of the sky. With this built-in automation, the pilot's duty is fast changing from that of flying to monitoring all these grand devices. Hardly satisfying, and certainly not fun.

In considering how a pilot's job description has changed from the hands-on era to the current era of programming and monitoring computers, old timers suggest that today's pilots better be careful or they might program themselves out of a job. Today's airplane is smart; it will yell at you if you are near the terrain or if your airspeed becomes too slow or too fast, and the control yoke will startle crews by suddenly shaking if they fly outside the envelope. Who would want that? We don't have to go to the airport to be yelled at; and yet they still call it pilot error if something goes wrong.

I don't think there are many old aviators from the hands-on era who envy the pilots of these aerial transport yawners. There are a multitude of pilots flying the jets these days who haven't even had the privilege of getting scared. But things were different back then: crews flew for the pure enjoyment of flying, and getting paid was an added joy. It was pilot ability (with occasional help from an unseen source according to Captain Ririe) that got them home safely.

During the exciting span of forty years, including its early history of chronicled triumphs and adventures flying the Rockies, Frontier had transformed from the old recips into the jet era flying Boeing 737s, and the McDonald/Douglas Dash 80s. Frontier had disposed of its B-727s for the more suited B-737. Then came the deregulation edict that sentenced many carriers to a slow death. Pan American World Airways, Eastern, Braniff, and other prominent carriers suffered from the malignant tentacles of this giant killer that began its initial plunder on the carriers in 1978. Frontier, after carrying a total of 87 million passengers to over 100 cities spread across the United States, Canada, and Mexico was slowly brought to the ground. Almost six-thousand employees sadly watched as Frontier slowly folder her wings in 1986 and relinquished her proud heritage to the corporate wars that were the nemesis of many airlines who were either swallowed or spit out by large conglomerates. A new carrier based in Denver and using the name

Frontier Airlines is not to be mistaken with the old, historical Frontier Airlines.

How It Was

The imported Fokker tri-motors were the first of the more convenient passenger aircraft to be used in the United States until disaster struck on March 31, 1931. The ensuing investigation revealed that interior wing rot had caused the aircraft to come apart in the air. Notre Dame football coach Knute Rockne was among the victims on the F-10.

The first practical passenger planes produced by the United States in the mid 1920s were the Ford, Boeing, and Stinson tri-motors. The beautiful twin-engined Curtiss Condor biplane served with American Airlines into the thirties. They were all slow, noisy and uncomfortable, but served well until 1933 when the first truly modern passenger plane, the Boeing 247, made its debut. The 247's low wing construction and mounted twin engines with retractable landing gear gave it a higher cruising speed than the old tri-motors.

It is interesting to follow the histories of the various airlines as they maneuvered to be the first to fly the most advanced aircraft that came off the assembly lines. United thought the Boeing 247 would be the new generation of aircraft with passenger acceptance, but its days became numbered with the evolution of the DC-3 that enjoyed a more comfortable cabin with twice as many seats. Having had a lock on all the new 247s being produced, United had to do some fast scrambling to get in line with other airlines for the new DC-3.

The DC-3 was named one of the 100 "best designed products." She first flew in 1935. Besides being a winner from day one, she was the first truly modern passenger plane providing spacious comfort. In the early days of passenger flying, she was the one that literally lifted many airlines off the ground. She was the first to make a profit from flying only passengers. She could cruise at 180 mph, a speed faster than most military fighters could then fly. For passenger comfort she had soundproofing as well as interior heating, and most important, she could fly weather safely.

In the thirties, Tommy Thompson, who was the proprietor of Thompson Flying Service in Salt Lake City, was one of the nation's early DC-3 pilots. Tommy was flying below the scud that was hanging over the San Francisco–Oakland Bay area. In one sudden motion, the DC-3 nosed down and impacted the bay. (In this modern age, this would be classified as a collision with the earth.) The ensuing investigation revealed that a microphone had fallen into the uncovered well area at the base of the yoke and lodged at its backside. Unable to pull the yoke back, or to dislodge the microphone in time to avoid hitting the water, Tommy and his copilot perished.

This was a simple mishap that turned into a major catastrophe. A cover was placed at the base of the yoke on all similar aircraft, preventing any repeat occurrences. This story is an example of many such episodes that befell the industry in the early days. Today's manufacturers, learning from and solving these past problems, now have a transportation system that we can fly with confidence.

In the Great Plains states with their low elevations, the DC-3 was like the new girl in town. In the high-density air she would kick up her heels, and the difference in her performance at lower elevations compared to the higher mountain elevations was incredible. Frontier pilots didn't envy the various airline crews flying the flatlands, but they were envious of all that extra power available from their engines.

To those who flew and labored to care for her, it was a fulfillment of love. To crews all over the world she became known as the "Grand Ol' Lady" for her dependability and for the affection felt by those acquainted with her. She hauled paratroopers and towed gliders in WWII. In the Southwest Pacific she became known as the biscuit transporter. She fought in Korea, Vietnam, and other wars. She flew rescue missions and went behind enemy lines to drop intelligence personnel. Knowingly overgrossed by her crews, she carried thousands of war refugees to safety and dropped emergency supplies to stranded victims in the Arctic and Antarctic. She hauled bailed hay for snow-stranded cattle and sheep. When the call went out for a reliable transporter, she was always there. No aircraft ever built came near to fulfilling the varied missions she was called upon to fly. And there was even a marriage performed on board. There isn't a pilot alive who flew her, who hasn't expressed his gratitude for having had the privilege of flying this old renowned workhorse.

They Endured

In my fledgling years I was privileged to have served with prime
captains, and a bonus to me it was. I felt as though I'd been paroled to
an airman's utopia flying with these veteran captains; many who had
flown long before the outbreak of WWII. After serving in the military,
many chose to remain flying by seeking employment with the various
airlines. Those who chose to come aboard one of the three predecessors
of Frontier were a special breed. It was said that the DC-3s would not
survive the first winter flying in the heart of the mountain empire. But
these highly qualified and experienced pilots tackled the elements over
the rock pile with determination. They endured scathing blizzards,
mountain waves, mountain turbulence and became confirmed believers
in the reputation of the Rocky Mountains. They flew throughout some
of the highest and most rugged terrain in this country.

There were none better and they knew it. However, as these veteran
pilots reached the FAA mandatory retirement age of sixty, they were
forced out of the cockpit. By approximately 1983, there were few
veteran WWII pilots still flying for the airlines. Nearly all of the
Frontier captains who served from the early DC-3 flights had each
logged over 30,000 hours. These dedicated pilots who had asked for
little and gave so much deserved a better hand from the FAA than what
was dealt to them.

10

Do You Need a No-Good Copilot?

Captain Ken Dealy and Captain Jack Kettler

It was a cold morning in February 1949 when Captain Ken Dealy shut down the engines in Cheyenne, Wyoming and walked into the small terminal in search of a mechanic. He was advised that it was the mechanic's day off but that there was a pilot in the coffee shop that might be helpful. That pilot/mechanic turned out to be Jack Kettler, a tall good-looking cowboy who had been a mechanic for Inland Air Lines and a copilot for Western Airlines. He was laid off by Western when business fell off and Kettler tells what happened next.

When I learned Captain Dealy's DC-3 had a stuck throttle, I agreed to take look at it, but since I didn't have my tools with me I needed two bits. I dug into my pocket and came up with the quarter I needed to remove the cowling from the engine. After a quick inspection I asked the captain to retard the throttle. Captain Dealy was apprehensive it might break the cable until I informed him there was a small sandstone rock stuck in the bell crank mounted on the firewall. By closing the throttle it crushed the rock that had flipped upward into the bell crank from the tire, and the DC-3 was ready for service.

After the logbook sign off, Captain Dealy told me to get ten dollars from the station manager. I told him, "I don't want your money, but do you need a no-good copilot for that operation?" I informed the captain of my past flying experience and the various aircraft I had flown in WWII, and that I was currently serving with the Wyoming Air Guard 187th Fighter Squadron in Cheyenne. Captain Dealy said, "You be here at 1800 when I make the return trip. Chief Pilot Scott Keller is coming through with me this evening." I was hired on the spot by the chief and told to be in Salt Lake City two weeks later on March 1, 1949.

The big, likable cowboy from Wyoming was everybody's friend and he didn't take *no guff* from anyone.

Kettler laughs when he tells that after he had been flying for two years, he was called into the chief pilot's office and told he had never filled out an application for employment. "So I filled out the papers and they said I was hired." Kettler received a recall from Western Airlines but elected to remain with Challenger. His reasons: "Our airline was one of the best and we had a group of people to work with that was like a big family. We busted our butts to make it one of the best."

Taming the Mustang

Flying copilot for Captain Kettler I learned that he was the sort of person who cared for the welfare of others, and he encouraged and helped many fledgling pilots in their early careers. For a big, rough Wyoming cowboy, he had a gentle heart and was considerate of his fellow men. I surmised he had already experienced a lifetime of close calls that he was reluctant to talk about. I knew he had some close calls while flying the B–24 and others, but I never did get the full story from him.

He related the following experience that took place in 1948 while still flying the P–51 for the Wyoming Guard. While doing some maintenance for the operator at the Lusk, Wyoming Airport, they had hangar-talked him into flying the P–51 to Lusk to make a few passes over the airport:

I peeled off and made an inverted pass over the airport. After I rolled upright and had pulled the nose up to regain altitude, I realized my legs and the lower portion of my body were saturated with some kind of fluid. I thought I might have a coolant leak but the engine temperature was in the green and the engine was responding well.

At this time I had quite a bit of altitude and was wearing my oxygen mask on 100% demand. I lifted the mask a little from my face and exclaimed, "Ma, someone left the gate open!" It was gasoline. There was a lot of dust blowing on the surface from the high wind, which changed my mind about bailing out. I pushed over into a power-off descent and opened the canopy slowly to remove the fumes from the cockpit. In the meantime the cockpit dried out so I elected to continue to Cheyenne. I didn't dare call on the radios, and wagging my wings they gave me a green light and I planted the P-51 on the tarmac.

What went wrong? At the bottom of the cockpit, there are two fuel quantity gauges, one on each side. I discovered the fuel gaskets had critically deteriorated to the extent that when flying inverted, they let gas flow out of the fuel gauges. Later the Lusk airport manager said, "You really had that P-51 smoking—you were going so fast you were leaving vapor trails." I said, "Frank, those vapor trails were from gasoline." He shook his head and commented that I lead a charmed life.

In relating this history to me, Jack said he couldn't understand how he made it out of that crisis. He commented, "Tex, I do believe in my lifetime I have been awfully lucky."

In rationalizing this incident, there was a lot more involved than just luck. Captain Kettler followed all the proper procedures to bring this to a survivable conclusion.

Black Night at Alamosa

The airport elevation in Alamosa, Colorado is 7,535 feet. Winters are cold and low-hanging clouds on the mountains extended out into the valley. All crews gave their undivided attention when descending into what some pilots called the hell hole approach. Crews continually double-checked their position and altitude when descending into the San Luis Valley surrounded by peaks extending to 14,390 feet. This was no utopia for the crews fighting the turbulence caused by gusty winds following the contours of the terrain. More than one crew had to break off their approach to one runway and switch to another as the squirrelly winds changed directions. It was a particularly black night when the DC-3 (with Captain Jack Kettler taking care of the copilot duties and copilot George Graham manipulating the controls) were making a VOR approach into Alamosa. Kettler tells the story:

We had completed the procedure turn and marked the time as we passed over the VOR inbound for the runway. The runway lies more than five-and-a-half miles from the VOR. We continued the letdown with a time fix to break out of the clouds and see the runway. Graham called out, "We have a red flag on the VOR, I'll continue the approach using the ADF."

We anxiously watched for the runway lights to make their appearance through the clouds. When we needed it the most, the ADF navigational facility failed. With no operative navigational facilities to guide us in the search for the airport, we continued with the approach while relying on the compass. Turbulent clouds held us in their grip as we waited with apprehension to break out and see the lights of the runway. The clock was telling us our time to see the runway was running out. I saw a couple of runway lights and called for Graham to take her down, "I have the lights."

We completed the gear-down check as Graham eased the DC-3 down through the clouds and with grateful feelings we heard the call of the runway as the wheels touched down on the windswept strip. As the tail settled down so did our hearts, but then the airport lighting facilities immersed into the black landscape leaving only the landing lights of the DC-3 to mark the runway. If the runway lights had blacked out thirty seconds sooner, we would have been in trouble. We slowly worked the DC-3 to the terminal in the black of night and shut down the weary engines. There had been a total power failure at the airport. Under the present circumstances it was impossible to call dispatch in Denver and notify them of our safe arrival. I suggested to the station manager that he contact the highway patrol and have them relate to dispatch in Denver of our safe arrival in Alamosa. We reclined in the cabin seats with the passengers for a much-needed rest and waited for the power to be restored to the airport.

DC-3 crews flying blind at adrenalin-pumping altitudes in the San Luis Valley surrounded by high mountains with navigational aids INOP would have as much chance of surviving as a horse thief standing before a hanging judge.

Steel Mill Approach at Provo

A widespread storm system covered the mountain states. Kettler, who was pulling gear for Captain Sam Grande at that time, relates they departed Albuquerque at a late hour for Salt Lake City with scheduled stops at Farmington, New Mexico and Grand Junction, Colorado:

> *We had planned to take on extra fuel at Farmington in view of the weather conditions at Grand Junction. Our present fuel load would sustain us only to Grand Junction with enough alternate fuel on board to continue to Vernal, Utah, plus an hour reserve.*
>
> *As we approached Farmington, we were advised the airport was below minimums with snow and sleet. Grand Junction weather was still holding so we continued on. When in range of Junction we were advised snow and sleet had obscured the southeast portion of the airport, and within a matter of minutes the airport would be entirely obscured.*
>
> *The strong surface wind was still holding out of the northwest which prevented us from shooting an ILS (instrument landing system). Unable to land straight in on runway 11 because of the strong tailwind, and with the lowering clouds preventing us from making a circling approach to land into the wind, we had no choice but to bypass Junction. Fuel was now becoming a critical factor. We had feeble hopes of trying for Vernal, Utah, but were informed the entire Uintah Basin was socked in. With reluctance we continued on with only enough fuel to reach Salt Lake City—with no reserves.*
>
> *Almost an hour later, flying over the Spanish Fork H-marker located forty-nine miles southeast of Salt Lake, we contacted dispatch at the Salt Lake airport. Our expectation took a further downturn when we were informed the visibility at Salt Lake City was now zero in fog. With fuel gauges registering zero on all three tanks, there were decisions to be made. An emergency would be declared and if we could make it to Salt Lake, we would attempt a blind landing on the runway.*
>
> *Continuing on to intercept the airway leading into Salt Lake, I yelled, "Sam! I can see the Provo steel mill directly below us, and the north boundary of the Provo airport."*

Provo did not have instrument landing facilities, so I advised dispatch we were going to make a steel mill approach into Provo. Sam made a nice spiraling descent through the large hole caused by heat from the steel mill. We could barely make out the threshold of runway 13 with the remainder obscured in fog. Sam banked the DC-3 around until we were on final for the runway, and after flying the last portion in scud, he planted the old girl onto the mist-shrouded runway.

It took twenty minutes taxiing in the fog before we could locate the ramp at the fixed base operations. It was past midnight and the office was deserted. Off to one side the little terminal still remained from when Challenger once served Provo. Luckily, Sam still carried a key. Inside we found the old company radio and called dispatch at Salt Lake, informing Mitchell that Fat and Omar had safely landed.

Because of a medical disability, Captain Kettler retired in 1981 after a career of thirty-two years flying for Challenger/Frontier. He resides in Manville, Wyoming, sixty miles east of Casper, Wyoming. As the mayor of Manville, Captain Kettler says his city, like all large cities, is suffering from exploding growth problems. At last count the population had increased to one hundred citizens.

11

On the Beam

Hauling passengers and mail has been a tradition in our family. My genealogy goes back to an age when some of my ancestors were pirates. They hauled anything that happened to come their way. So one way or another, many in the family have chosen various modes of transportation from sea-going vessels, the Overland Stage, pony express, passenger mail trains, to the airlines to make their livelihood. Wherever it came from, my desire to fly an airplane was bigger than I was.

Unfortunately, I did not fly while serving in the military in WWII, and all I had to offer in multi-engine experience was training time in a surplus UC-78 twin-engine Cessna, known as the bamboo bomber, and a Twin Beech C-45—hardly competition for the surplus of pilots available after the war. But perseverance paid off. I wanted to fly out west in the Rocky Mountain region, so I camped on the doorstep of Frontier Airlines until Chief Pilot Scott Keller finally relented and let me in the door.

How well I remember my initial training. After passing an acceptance test and completing ground school in Denver, I was sent to Salt Lake City to complete my Link and flight training in the DC-3. The Link trainer was a ground training device that simulated flight conditions; it was the same trainer in which many WWII pilots received their instrument training. It had stubby wings mounted on each side of a cockpit to make it look like an airplane, and a box-type hood that swung down and covered the cockpit to simulate instrument conditions. The cockpit rested on a mixed contrivance of mechanisms and bellows that gave it motion.

Captain Jack Kettler was the Link instructor then. When he asked what type of radio orientation I would prefer to use, I requested the low frequency range approach. He seemed somewhat surprised and commented, "I thought that went the way of the old wood and fabric aircraft. But if you can find your way to the runway using that old method of navigation, you won't have any trouble with the newer VOR." (visual omni range)

With the hood down and the instrumentation lights turned up, I was fired up to go. Suddenly the hood went up and a perplexed voice said, "Here, you forgot these." As he handed over my earphones I must have looked a little bewildered, and with some assurance Kettler commented, "Hang in there, you aren't even off the ground yet."

After practicing climbs, descents, and steep turns, I began to feel a little more confident in the ulcer box. Kettler asked if I had the earphones on and the low-frequency radio tuned to the Salt Lake Range Station. I assured him everything was on and tuned. "All right," he said, "locate your present position, and then shoot the approach into the Salt Lake Airport." I struggled through the ninety-degree method of orientation and located the approach beam of the north range leg. After bracketing the steady hum of the beam, I continued inbound on the published heading of 149 degrees to track the steady tone of the on-course aural signal. Turning the volume control down, I listened for the increase in volume of the steady tone that would verify I was inbound to the range station. If the aircraft drifts a little right of course, the steady aural tone (bi-signal zone) will begin to fade and the Morse code letter "A," expressed by an aural tone of "dit-da," will become more audible. If the aircraft drifts left of course, the letter "N," expressed as "da-dit," will become more audible, and the steady on-course tone will fade until it is inaudible unless a corrective course change is initiated to capture the steady tone.

There is an old saying, "Let the humming of the angels lead you to that safe haven." After a cross-country flight navigating by their ears, the early-day aviators staggered around on the ground waiting for the humming of the angels in their ears to subside.

Using my ears to navigate, I managed to hold the steady tone until I was over the cone of silence, which is the indication you are over the low-frequency radio-range tower. From there I flew the published heading to the runway and marked the time estimate it would take to reach the runway. Descending to the minimum approach altitude (altitude above the surface), and at the estimated time to break out and see the runway, the hood remained down. (This indicated I was still in clouds.) Not seeing the runway, I began executing the missed approach. The hood on the little Link trainer suddenly raised up and Captain Kettler growled, "I left the hood down to simulate you were still in the clouds. You didn't ask for weather information to determine the height of the cloud base. If you had, you would have known the bases of the clouds were below minimums and you wouldn't break out and have visual contact with the runway." After a lengthy period of one-sided verbal gestures and several more sessions in the ulcer box, I was cleared for flight training in the DC-3.

Chief Pilot Scott Keller is a patient instructor. I had studied hard and felt I had memorized the systems and every part and size of the DC-3. During the walk-around the first question he asked was, "What is the tire pressure in the mains?" I stood there like a frozen rope. "The tire pressure in the mains?" "Yes," the chief replied, "the tire pressure in the mains." My confidence took a downturn; I couldn't even answer the first question. I suppose chief Keller could see the perspiration running down my neck and, not wanting to fly around with a clammy student in the cockpit, asked, "What is the military designation for the DC-3?" I hurriedly answered, "C-47." The chief smiled and asked again, "What is the tire pressure?" It dawned on me he was giving a strong reference, so I blurted out, "Forty seven." He said, "You got it and don't forget it." And I never did.

Taxiing the DC-3 for the first time was about as easy as convincing a nervous jackrabbit to walk a straight line. That lady had the touchiest brakes in the whole world: you just think about applying them and they grab you. After getting it down to a fishtail ride down the taxiway, Keller commented, "If we had passengers aboard, they would all be stacked in the aisle, but don't sweat it, it's a well known axiom that the Grand Ol' Lady is a bit contrary on the ground." He instructed me in how to fan the rudder and smooth up the ride. On the takeoff roll, as the tail rises the nose lowers. It was frustrating to see the runway rising up, but I bluffed it out and pretended not to notice the odd sensation of sinking into the runway. After a hard session of climbs, descents, sixty-degree banked turns and stalls, Keller said, "We'll shoot several landings to get you up to speed and more accustomed to the landing temperament of the DC-3. In the air she's docile, but on the ground it takes a pilot to master her."

On my first approach the old control tower, then situated on the east side, cleared us to land north on the north–south runway. The landing was so unpleasant—more like a controlled crash. It didn't do a lot for my morale when the control tower began offering Captain Keller odds the Grand Ol' Lady wouldn't survive another encounter with the earth, and I felt even worse when he didn't take them up on it. Then they suggested it would be better for all concerned if they cleared us to our landing approach to the south. In making our approach over the less-populated boundaries, there wouldn't be so many spectators. Keller happily agreed.

After becoming oriented to looking through a windshield almost seventeen feet above the asphalt, and a lot of body language from the chief, I was able to convince the old girl not to swap ends and to safely stay in the confines of the runway without crashing and burning—much to my relief and that of Captain Keller. But again I had an odd sensation after touchdown as the tail started to sink to the runway, the nose of the DC-3 began to rise as though we were lifting off again. Not wanting the chief to know I was sitting across the pedestal from him and feeling sensationalized, I put on my game face and hung in there. Having been given these numbers in ground school, the significance of it never dawned on me until experiencing it in the DC-3. When the tail rises for take off, the nose lowers two feet. As the tail lowers to the runway after landing, the cockpit rises two feet.

With the hood obscuring my outside view there were several more grinding sessions of shooting the different instrument approaches with various equipment failures to simulate emergencies that could befall an unsuspecting pilot. From the grinding training the chief was laying on me, I thought maybe he didn't like me. But when I got into the real world of flying the mountain empire I understood why. The chief assured himself that his crews exceeded the safety requirements of the CAA (Civil Aeronautics Administration) and Frontier for the isolated airports they would be flying into in the mountain empire. He insisted they keep a high priority in practicing simulated approaches using the dated manual-loop orientation to establish a time-distance to the radio fix and then to track an inbound course to the runway with a partial panel (minimum flight instruments). After completing flight training checks, I was given an oral exam on the DC-3 as well as the route structure. Notified I had successfully completed the copilot requirement checks was another step towards the final goal I'd dreamed of as a youth.

I mentioned to Captain Dave Cannon that I finally figured out why the chief had laid it on me in training: "It was because he wanted to keep me around." The captain answered, "It wasn't you he was concerned about, it was the DC-3s."

First Scheduled Copilot Trip

With the completion of my line observation trips, I was cleared to fly the line as a first officer. One of my first line trips stands out as though it was yesterday. Arriving at the crew room in my new uniform to fill out the flight plan, I was happy to learn I would be flying with Captain Jack Kettler, who was responsible for getting me up to speed in the Link trainer.

Departing Salt Lake City I was busier than a grizzly bear who had sat on a hornets' nest. I had to remember the procedure for manipulating the gear, read the checklist out loud, and set the climb power on both engines without getting them out of sync, all while watching out for other traffic and trying to communicate with Salt Lake Departure and the company radio at the same time. Who said this flying was a piece of cake?

When we approached Rock Springs the radio informed us the main east–west runway was closed for the new overlay, so we landed northeast on the shorter northeast–southwest runway. We made a one-engine stop (only one engine was shut down to save time on the ground). After exchanging MPX we proceeded on to Frontier's small hub in Riverton, Wyoming where MPX was exchanged with flights from Billings, Montana and Denver. After a quick turnaround we returned to a windy Rock Springs for the second time that morning. The agents hustled to exchange the sorted cargo and get us out on time. Climbing into the Wyoming skies we picked up a heading for Vernal, Utah. I was behind the power curve, but with patience from Captain Kettler, I was feeling more assured about this flying business, but soon I didn't feel so good. Twenty miles south of Rock Springs the right engine let go with a vengeance and began to shake and snort so unmercifully that Captain Kettler had to shut it down.

With a full load of passengers and a heavy cargo of Howard Hughs' oil drilling bits, we were grossed out in weight. That and the high airport elevation at Rock Springs, just under 7,000 feet, added up to a higher ground speed during the approach and a higher touchdown speed—not a good situation for the northeast landing we planned on the northeast–southwest runway. Landing on runway three would have the good engine upwind for better directional stability on the runway. With no other alternatives and forced to make a single-engine landing in a crosswind that was gusting to 25 mph out of the northwest, Captain Kettler would have his piloting skills tested.

The captain fought to make the turn back to the airport in the rough air and clear the high terrain at the same time. High hills and valleys surround the Rock Springs airport causing turbulence. Even with a calm wind at Rock Springs, the air is turbulent. The captain commented, "They should use a log chain instead of a windsock." After lining up for a straight-in approach we listened to Rock Springs radio advise to watch for equipment alongside the runway. The outside temperature was in the high 80s and the moderate turbulence at the lower altitudes, caused by high surface winds over the terrain, was beginning to strain the seams of my unruffled composure. Captain Kettler had the throttle to the firewall on the remaining engine, but she kept losing altitude in the hot, turbulent air. The captain, his jaw set, had a look of determination that this old gal was going to get us down in one piece come hell or high water (not seeing any water I knew it was going to be hell). "As bad as she wants to land we need to keep her head up and pointed to the runway," he said. He asked me to check the location of the equipment alongside the runway.

"Mercy! It's a bulldozer," I cried, "and it's in the middle of the runway about two-thirds of the way down." Kettler replied, "We have no choice, drop the gear and complete the checklist." With the turbulent air bouncing the old gal all over the threshold, we touched down on the edge of the strip. Kettler stomped full right rudder and held full left aileron with a touch of power on the upwind engine to keep her straight down the runway. Approaching the mid intersection of the east–west runway, we didn't seem to be slowing much. I now could see the windsock whipping on its staff showing a wind shift indicating it was now coming from the west, giving us a quarterly tailwind. Kettler was aware of the wind shift. He yelled, "I may have to ground loop." Ahead of us I could see several construction workers headed for the boonies. I can still hear the screech of the tires as Kettler fought to end the flight in one piece. She was losing headway, but with the dozer growing in size it didn't appear she could stop in time. Kettler was poised to ground loop, but he held his course and we slid to a stop 75 yards short of the bulldozer. The Captain hurdled from the cockpit—I suppose he had something to say to the bulldozer operator. After the excitement was over, Kettler said, "The priest we had on board saved us." The priest replied, "Captain Kettler saved us." As for me and my maiden trip, all I wanted to do was go home.

12

The Reluctant Phantom

Captain Bob Rich remembers a time in the late 1940s when he was pulling gear for Captain Sam Grande and they were flying into Kemmerer, Wyoming, a centralized location for the coal strip mines, oil and gas fields, and large fossil beds. Absaroka Ridge bordered the community to the west and north with elevations up to 8,000 feet. Without a navigational facility, airline crews would take bearings off the old Fort Bridger range station to find their way in inclement weather. The airport with its high elevation of almost 7,300 feet would at most times suffer from strong westerly winds. Inasmuch as the airport was an open grass area, the crews would just aim into the wind and plant the DC-3 onto the grass.

> **Captain Bob Rich:** *A small wooden structure served as the terminal building. Our curiosity was aroused as to why this small building always had a log chain tethered to it. Then the day came when Fat and Skinhead (Captain Grande and Bob) landed in a strong westerly and taxied to our customary parking, only to find the terminal building had absconded. The answer as to the log chain soon manifested itself as we watched a large truck dragging the reluctant building back through the stiff wind to its proper location.* [end quote style]

Blind Landing

Retired Captain Bob Rich says that society as a whole will be unable to relate to the conditions of that era, and is aware that stories told by us old airmail pilots will sound like embellished ludicrous allegations. "However," he says, "they are true."

> *I vividly recall departing Grand Junction, Colorado on a night flight to Salt Lake City, in a very marginal weather situation. It was shortly before*

Christmas in the 1950s. A front had developed northwest of Salt Lake City. The forecast didn't show it as a serious threat to our route of flight. If we stayed on the ground every time they forecast a weather disturbance, we would never accomplish much in the transportation of passengers and goods. Flying the high mountains with their varied weather patterns was a challenge Frontier pilots wrestled with daily.

First Officer Richard Ure and I opined that weather conditions and the forecast offered a successful completion of this journey. The weather at the Salt Lake air terminal was adequate for dispatch. We therefore enplaned passengers and departed.

En route, unbeknownst to us (the information wasn't relayed) the front accelerated and we penetrated it in the vicinity of the Duchesne, Utah, H-marker beacon. Our relatively benign winds aloft suddenly increased to an extremely strong headwind (later determined to be in excess of 100 mph). Grand Junction (our alternate) went below minimums. Vernal, Utah was down so we were committed to Salt Lake City.

We were enjoying headwinds, prop and wing ice to a degree much more than we had anticipated, and our ground speed had deteriorated to less than 100 mph. Salt Lake weather in the interim had gone to zero ceiling and zero visibility with heavy snow. Hoping for improved weather in Salt Lake, we continued on. Fuel reserve was a very important consideration at this point and we were aware that we probably would have one shot, and one shot only, at Salt Lake City.

We departed the Spanish Fork H-marker en route to intercept the localizer of the instrument landing system at the fan marker. Ordinarily it required approximately 11 minutes to accomplish this transition. After approximately twenty minutes we intersected the localizer at the marker. It was obvious that we were involved in a situation that was extremely distressful. Because of the low altitude jet stream, we were conscious of the fact that our aircraft was running very low on fuel on our approach to the Salt Lake Airport.

With the weather at the Ogden, Utah airport reporting zero/zero conditions, Rock Springs, Wyoming was our new paper "alternate." The remaining fuel would not sustain us to Rock Springs. We elected to continue the approach. The Salt Lake tower advised that the weather was zero/zero. I implored the tower operator to give us minimums on the weather so we could legally attempt an approach. He stated that **in his opinion**, bless his heart, the ceiling was 200 feet and visibility was one-half mile. This enabled us to shoot the approach without a lot of paperwork.

Established on the glide path of the ILS (instrument landing system), I moved up and down gingerly to convince myself that the facility was operating properly. At 500 feet I requested that First Officer Ure to monitor our approach as far as any possible visual reference was concerned. At minimums (200 feet above the surface) he stated, "Automobile headlights seemed to have passed beneath us."

Without ever seeing the runway we contacted the surface on about four inches of powdery snow, probably my best landing ever. Dick Ure yelled, "If you were a girl, I'd kiss you." Approximately twenty minutes later, in poor visibility caused by fog and heavy snow, we taxied up to the old east terminal.

Private Stateroom

During one DC-3 flight from Gallup, New Mexico to Albuquerque, the stew came to the cockpit and informed me that a lady passenger was in the blue room and the door was stuck shut:

With screwdriver in hand I knocked on the stuck door and asked the lady if she was all right. She replied, "I will be when I can return to my seat." I informed her I would have her out in a jiffy. I pried and twisted, pulled and cussed, but the door would not open. It was going to be a long jiffy.

Knowing it was illegal for the blue room to be occupied during landing, but not wanting to force entry and delay the departing trip from Albuquerque while repairs were made, I asked if she would mind remaining in the blue room until after our arrival. She said, "I prefer to be someplace other than here, but under the circumstances I have little choice." I advised the stew not to say anything of our difficulty and matters would be taken care of on the ground.

After disembarking the passengers, a mechanic came aboard and dislodged the door, releasing the lady. I attempted to apologize, but she laughingly cut me off. "I enjoyed my own private stateroom," she said, "but that seat needs a cushion on it."

The Shredded Blouse

Approaching the high country en route to Flagstaff, Arizona from Phoenix, the stew stepped into the cockpit and said, "I have a problem." I said, "Yes, it is rather obvious." The front of her blouse was soaked with coffee. She explained that a passenger was handing over his half-empty cup of cold *coffee when the DC-3 lurched in the rough air, and he ended up throwing all the contents on her blouse.*

Being the gentleman I am, I asked her to give me her blouse and I would have it dried off in thirty seconds. I opened my side window and held the blouse out to dry. With a painful look I withdrew the remnant—a few buttons and strips of tattered cloth. As the stew looked distressingly at what remained of her blouse, I commented, "Well, at least it's dry." I then reached back for my overnight bag, and the stew finished out the trip wearing my striped shirt.

Egg Head

Captain Bob Rich had hands that weaved all over the cockpit like a maestro leading the symphony. He could set up all the switches in the cockpit with a wave of his hand while you were still trying to locate the proper checklist. He never missed a beat or made a mistake. But, as he tells it, he did have a little trouble with an egg once:

In the 1940s and '50s it was nice to have a snack to tide you over on some of the long hauls in the DC-3. But unless you brought your own lunch there was nothing to eat except consommé soup. Tired of soup I was among those who would brown-bag it, and I always brought along something extra for a hungry copilot. Handing Dick Ure a hard-boiled egg, I said, "Have at it, Dick." Dick was a character in his own right and taking the egg, he cracked it on the top of his head. I was laughing until I saw raw egg running down the face and neck of my copilot. We both sobered up fast. I said, "I made a mistake." Copilot Ure, knowing there is not much you can tell a captain, didn't say anything. But with egg on his face, he was awarded the next landing.

As I think back to those days, I wouldn't trade them for any other period of time. We sometimes found it necessary to survive by our wits. Then you were an aviator that flew by the seat of your pants when all else had failed. My memories of this stimulating period in aviation and flying the DC-3 will always be with me. I frequently think back to that era when there was still romance in aviation to sustain me in these times. After retiring, I lived in Hawaii a number of years, and now settled in Littleton, Colorado. I'm just hanging around until it's my turn to go to that big hangar in the sky.

I asked Captain Rich at what point in life he made the decision to fly. He said, "There was no decision—I always knew I was going to fly." Captain Rich began flying in Chicago in 1938. He flew the old Fairchilds and a Waco with an OX5 mounted engine among others. During WWII he flew in the Army Air Corps Transport Command. Among the many fighters he flew, including the P-40, he particularly enjoyed flying the P-51 and the P-47. He flew most of the heavy bombers and spent considerable time flying the B-24. He flew all the medium bombers from the A-20 Boston/Havoc family, the B-25 Mitchell, Douglas A-26 Invader, and the B-26 Marauder.

The Marauder

Captain Rich remembers standing at attention with other cadets on the drill field when a formation of B-26s flew over. Before the entire viewing staff, one of the aircraft dropped out of formation, rolled over and spun to the ground. He says, "That didn't do much for my esprit de corps."

With Captain Rich's logs showing he had flown the B-26 Marauder, and delving into the history of this rare beauty, a short narrative of its flying characteristics might be enlightening to those not familiar with this bullet-like twin engine aircraft of which 4,115 were assembled by Martin.

As far back as when Pan American Air Ferries contracted overseas transporting of military aircraft, the B-26 Marauder was not popular with ferry crews. They were heavy planes with short wings that gave it a wing loading of nearly 50 pounds per square foot compared to the DC-3 wing loading of 25.5 pounds per square foot and seemed to have an unusually high rate of accidents—landing and taking off. The Pratt & Whitney R-2800s were the same engines used on Frontier Airlines CV-340s. Ferry crews called the Marauder "the flying prostitute." With its short wing span, it was said "it had no visible means of support." Others called it "the separator" meaning it separated the men from the boys. Yet others called it "the widow maker" or "the flying coffin."

More wing was added, but also more weight so the Marauder still was not popular with many of the crews who flew her. But she held an enviable record for her performance in WWII flown by proud crews who were given added proficiency training for her marginal flying characteristics. The last remaining Marauder in flying condition crashed in 1995 killing all on board. Of the several others that survive, one is in the USAF Museum near Dayton, Ohio and another located in the National Air & Space Museum in Washington. One or two others are in various stages of restoration on the West Coast.

After WWII, Captain Rich flew for the Flying Tigers from 1946 until 1948. He was employed by Challenger Airlines in June of 1948, and retired from Frontier in 1980. After pushing throttles for over thirty-two years for Frontier, Captain Rich was forced to vacate the front office because of the mandatory retirement age of sixty thought up by the FAA (Federal Aviation Administration). His logs totaled out at 30,700 hours in the sky.

13

I Never Got Tired of That

Captain George Graham describes the following from his notes
of ingrained memories flying the difficult and challenging routes
throughout the mountain empire:

*Many times we earned every cent of our pay; and then there were flights
that had us sitting on top of the world viewing large scrolls of magnificent
landscapes unfolding before us. I never got tired of that. The Grand Ol'
Lady had you down there where you could see everything close up sitting in
the best seats in the house. The jets are nice but they'll never come close to
the DC-3 in offering breathtaking views of nature at its best. In those days
passengers had their noses pressed to the windows. Now they read a book.*

*How well I remember the years when we took off from Denver at dawn
on the first leg of trip 31. When departing Pueblo (it seems like only
yesterday), we had to convince the DC-3 to make a max climb effort to
clear the backbone of the Continental Divide. In the cool mountain air we
skimmed through the eminent Monarch Pass (the airline's namesake) while
we continually surveyed the high terrain with suspicion. Our adrenaline
kept us alert to counter any assault this pass was notorious for. Counting
seven peaks north we could see the lofty Mt. Elbert, the highest peak in
Colorado at 14,431 feet. I was never without awe watching these numerous
peaks slide by my side window.*

*After exiting Monarch Pass at its western extremity, I would ease the
throttles back to begin a slow let down to lower elevations in an attempt
to give our passengers' ears more time to adjust. Proceeding on to the
small airport at Gunnison, navigating was only a matter of maneuvering
between the high, steep slopes of the canyon. From Gunnison we continued
to Montrose, Colorado, and then to Grand Junction, our turn-around
terminus.*

On the return trip from Grand Junction, if the mountain passes east of Gunnison had become obscured in clouds, the flight was forced to divert to what was known as "the long way around." This alternate route provided H-markers for flying in inclement weather while making an end run through southern Colorado until we could turn northeast towards Denver. After clearing the high Chama pass, our course brought us to the Fort Garland H-marker that provided an invisible pathway into the confines of the towering La Veta pass.

Flying by the gauges, we had to carefully crank the coffee-grinder to tune in the La Veta H-marker. During the twenty-four-mile flight between Fort Garland and La Veta, our undivided attention was directed at the instruments, and we continually made sure our directional gyros and the azimuth for the ADF pointers were aligned with the compass as we maneuvered through the narrow divide obscured in clouds. If there was thunderstorm activity in the area, the precipitation would cause our ADF needles to become useless as they hunted and rotated about the azimuth face. We then reverted to the old manual loop form of navigation to guide us through the pass.

While flying the aircraft in turbulence with one hand, I would use the other hand to rotate the manual loop antenna to track the aural-null signals between the two H-markers. We experienced crosswinds in that pass that would cause a crab into the wind as much as thirty degrees or more to maintain our track, and with magnetic disturbances that caused the compass to swing, we never had time to be scared. But I'll say one thing, that pass was resplendent when we could observe the high panorama, but grossly offensive when mother nature had pulled a curtain across the entrance. Free from the environment of the Rocky Mountains, the ol' gal would put her head down as we headed for the home stretch.

Before the merger in 1950, stewards were assigned on all three of Frontier's predecessor airlines until Challenger began hiring stewardesses in July of 1948. Besides cabin duties the stewards had the added responsibility of entering compartment A (baggage/mail/cargo aft of cabin) during flight to check and rearrange mail sacks for the various stops, similar to what the old railroad mail agents used to do.

14

The Smoke Detector

Captain George Graham began his airline career in April of 1948 as a steward for Monarch Airlines based in Denver. Graham still laughs about a particular trip when he was serving as steward:

At the time, the DC-3 was at max climb performance to reach 13,000 feet in order to clear the Uncompahgre Plateau when I hurried aft to sort out the mail sacks before Compartment A (commonly known as "comp-A") became cold-soaked from the frigid temperatures awaiting us at the higher altitudes. When I turned the handle on the door to return to the warm inviting cabin, it wouldn't open. I thought about the long flight at 13,000 feet with no heat, and all the unattended passengers. I anxiously twisted the handle and pushed on the door to no avail. Not wanting to bust the door off its hinges for fear of upsetting the passengers (that's my story and I'm sticking to it), I lit a cigarette and pondered my predicament while sitting on the mail sacks.

My attention was drawn to the smoke detector that would signal the flight deck crew of smoke or fire in comp-A, and a plan soon evolved to end my imprisonment. Taking a long drag I inhaled deeply, then blew smoke into the detector. Not long after, a wild-eyed copilot yanked the door open to stare at me as I calmly sat on the mail sacks and smoked my cigarette. His first words, "Graham! What in hell are you doing?"

Later, the passengers informed me that when the call light lit up and there wasn't a response, the cockpit door flew open and a wild-eyed copilot rushed past them straight to the rear of the aircraft and after some exerted effort, flung the door open.

After I got the copilot calmed down and explained what had happened, his eyes gradually returned to a glassy expression that seemed to say, "Why me?" Shaking his head he returned to the cockpit. I can assure you that fire in flight is one of the most serious emergencies a crew can experience. Happily, this was a planned, false emergency, but the response was excellent.

Captain Graham served as a combat air crewman in a Navy patrol bomber during WWII. He used his GI education benefits to become an airline pilot. Well qualified, he was soon cleared to fly the right seat, and not long after was promoted to captain. He experienced a career full of the joys and trials flying the Rocky Mountains. Captain Graham gave many hundreds of hours to help improve our chances to maintain the safest airline record in the worldwide history of civil aviation as the chairman of the Air Line Pilots Association safety committee. In 1983 Graham was forced to leave at the retirement age of sixty after a thirty-five-year career with Monarch/Frontier. But after spending so many years in the front office of DC-3s and the jets that replaced them, he couldn't give it up; he continued on for another 9 ½ years flying for FedEx and UPS, and delivered mail for contract carriers. He served as a charter pilot and hauled freight and flew fire patrol. Many times he flew into the back country on medical evacuation missions. Now retired, this captain who has just about done it all, resides in Colorado.

15

Line Squalls

As a result of the decision made by the CAB (Civil Aeronautics Board) from hearings that involved the *Seven States* case, Frontier was awarded routes in the 1950s that extended from the Rocky Mountains eastward throughout the Great Plains region. Tornadoes are prevalent in that area; they are caused by cooler air rushing in from the northwest and colliding with warm, moist air that moves up from the southwest and ripens into a cauldron of boiling clouds causing havoc with anything in its path. This condition resulted in the name "tornado alley." Kansas spawns a mean annual tornado every 10,000 square miles, more than any other state.

Before the advent of airborne weather radar, there were chronicles of aircraft incurring structural failure from encounters with thunderstorms embedded in large cumulonimbus build-ups (although most cumulus clouds do not grow into thunderstorms). Flying solely on instruments in an environment of this nature can be catastrophic. You suddenly find yourself surrounded by hail, lightning, and updrafts with speeds that can exceed 6,000 feet per minute (it is suggested that the Grand Ol' Lady tangled with thunderstorms more than any other aircraft) or downdrafts that can exceed 2,500 feet per minute. Both of these, in close proximity, create a strong vertical shear and turbulent conditions that make an unfortunate soul offer a quick prayer if the elements give him time.

There are also first-hand accounts of pilots whose fate it was to run afoul of strong updrafts from the cumulus cycle of large mass-embedded thunderstorms. If they survived the encounter, they were sometimes spit out several thousand feet higher than where they went charging in. If an aircraft penetrates the cumulonimbus buildup during its mature stage, the crew is likely to find themselves on a fast elevator ride to purgatory.

Buckle your seatbelts for this. With no radar, one company DC-3 crew was making their night run from Denver to Omaha, picking their way through a corridor of the least minimal weather shown by lightning flashes. They swung southeast weaving between dark, towering cumulus clouds that loomed like giant pillars and through the gray white canyons to what they hoped would be a soft spot in the weather, but turned out to be what is called a "sucker hole" by pilots. (Without radar, there is no sure way to pick soft spots in a thunderstorm.) The crew felt their bodies pressed into the seat cushions as the Gs increased their initial upward boost, engulfing them in a slicing updraft that shot them toward the heavens. Then, abruptly, their laps strained against the seatbelts as they rode the vertical shear in its downward plunge only to be expelled out the side of the cumulonimbus where they found themselves engulfed in hail from the overhang of its anvil-like head.

The copilot held the logbook with its metal cover next to the captain's windshield to ward off the elements should they force entry into the cockpit from the constant onslaught of marble-sized hail. The thick-skinned DC-3 continued into Omaha with its white-knuckled crew with little wear and tear to show for its tornado alley encounter. Although a few swore never again, they always signed in for their next scheduled run.

Upgraded aircraft and the installation of radar on all passenger planes removed the shaky era of questionable decisions and the guesswork became a thing of the past. It was sheer pleasure to give a wide path to those destructive devices of Mother Nature. The phasing in of jet aircraft in the late fifties and early sixties enabled crews to fly above most of the build-ups, or go around them.

There could never be enough accolades bestowed on those aviators who flew pre-radar, pre-pressurized aircraft on a daily basis enduring all the destructive devices that Mother Nature disguised in clouds to hinder their flight paths. Retired Frontier Captain Bob Rich put it bluntly, "In those days our eyes were our radar and you couldn't force an airplane to do more than it was created to do. There are many aluminum scrap piles strewn over the landscapes by those who thought otherwise."

The most reliable weather reports available were those that crews shared with others while passing in flight. Captain Bob Rich was climbing through turbulent rain-sodden clouds after departing Jackson Hole, Wyoming. The inbound flight with Chief Pilot Scott Keller at the controls asked for the weather conditions in the Jackson Hole area. No one will ever know the reaction of our chief when he received Captain Rich's report, "Hell, I can see clear to the windshield."

Embedded Thunderstorms over the Wasatch

Captain Bob Rich: *In retrospect of flying the beloved Grand Ol' Lady, I'm reminded of what a durable lady she was. Captain Al Mooney and I were flying from New Mexico to Salt Lake City. We were in cloud the entire route. Approaching the Wasatch Mountains without radar to define the weather cells, we flew into an embedded thunderstorm, and were suddenly seized by a turmoil of furious air currents. Both engines were cutting out from the intermittent flow of fuel caused by the turbulence, and the gyros were tumbling so violently we were unable to read them.*

The ship was recovered from its downward plunge—still in clouds. Knowing the mountains were now towering above us, Captain Mooney opted for a south heading until we picked up the 106 degree relative bearing from the old Spanish Fork H-marker. We then tracked the inbound to the station on the 286 degree bearing through the narrow confines of a cloud-obscured canyon to the safety of Utah Valley (known as Happy Valley). Recovering our sanity, we landed safely in Salt Lake City. Yes, we were a little shook up.

The following day while talking with Captain Mooney, I commented that we were fortunate to be standing on Mother Earth all in one piece. With nerves steadied and a voice much calmer than on the previous day, he wisecracked, "Piece of cake." Then perhaps an awareness of realism kicked in after all the bravado. With that mischievous grin known as Captain Mooney's trademark he affirmed, "With all the instruments gyrating, I thought for a fleeting moment we were going to make the final payment on the farm."

Larry A. Ball, who authored the novel Those Incomparable Bonanzas, informed me that he keeps the control wheel of a DC-3 in his office as a conversation piece. He says, "If that wheel could talk, I'm sure it could tell quite a story. There are grooves from the pilots' tight hand grip plainly worn into the wheel." My wife said to tell Larry that all the armrests in the passenger cabin had even deeper grooves.

Burst Seams

Flying our scheduled route from Riverton, Wyoming to Salt Lake City with a planned, one-engine stop at Vernal, Utah, we approached the Uinta Mountains at their eastern extent near midnight. It was not a pleasant night. We were running late, slowed by the low, dark, moisture-laden clouds that covered the region. The cumulative moisture in the sodden air mass was intensifying for its escape through burst seams. St. Elmo's fire (a luminous discharge of electricity in weather) was fading from its dance around the windshield leaving a dark void in the night for my copilot and I to stare into. Finally free from entrapment, the rain descended in sheets. It seeped into the cockpit from around the windshield and through the seals of the overhead escape hatch and dribbled onto our headsets. With added power the Grand Ol' Lady struggled to maintain the assigned altitude of 13,000 feet over the high Uintas.

Because of the heavy, rainfed moisture, the ADF (automatic direction finder) was unable to home in on the low-powered H-marker at Vernal, nor were we able to make contact on the company radio; and, if the situation wasn't bad enough, the number one engine began to vibrate caused by excessive moisture in the ignition harness. Initiating a time-distance, our estimated position was thirty miles north of Vernal. After ten minutes and supposedly over the Vernal H-marker, there was still no radio contact with the station due to precipitation static interference.

The left engine was still complaining and the ADF needles were still refusing to home on Vernal, leaving us no navigational fix to make the approach down through the storm. We bypassed Vernal and picked up a DH (dead reckoning heading) for the Duchesne, Utah H-marker. As we approached from approximately twenty miles out, the ADF needles began to settle down and home in on the Duchesne H-marker. Shortly after, we broke into the clear and continued to Salt Lake City. We were safe but the same storm that we escaped left tragedy on the ground beneath us. The following day, newspapers reported that a flood caused by heavy rains racing through Sheep Creek Canyon had drowned seven campers.

I couldn't help but wonder if they had heard the DC-3 as she struggled over the rain-drenched canyon that fateful hour.

Bird Strike

Nearing Salt Lake City, the Grand Ol' Lady was high-railing it along the airways like a 4-8-4 steam locomotive headed for the roundhouse. She was flying at 14,000 feet between dense cloud layers with the lower layer extending to the surface. Midnight was drawing near and it was blacker than Sadie's biscuits. With total darkness outside, we kept busy monitoring the instruments and listening to the mesmerizing throb of the Twin Wasp engines. Then I heard it. I couldn't identify what it was. It wasn't loud, but I heard something outside my sliding window. You become immune to the odd sounds the engines sometimes make. I've often thought they dream up little burps and misses just to keep you awake. But then, the Grand Ol' Lady doesn't really have a soul, or does she?

But I had heard something, so after landing at Salt Lake City, I told the mechanic about the incident. Together we walked around the aircraft with a flashlight to see if we could find anything. There it was, just outboard of the number one engine. The leading edge of the wing had an impression in it about the size of a basketball. On closer inspection, there were a couple of feathers stuck in dried blood. The DC-3 had struck a large bird. Unbelievable: a bird at 14,000 feet in the middle of the night flying between cloud layers. I felt bad for it. We couldn't identify what kind it was, but if birds are going to begin using the airways, the FAA will probably require them to have an airways clearance from air traffic control.

Fireball in the Night Skies

March had gone out like a lion, and in the cool April evening, it was a pleasure to look up and see the stars in the clear night air. Twilight had made its departure over the western horizon, and although the black night had settled in, we had unlimited visibility as we watched with interest the isolated lights scroll beneath us in the deep canyons of the Wasatch Range.

After leveling off at 11,500 feet, and the ol' gal was on the step in the smooth night air, Captain Ririe eased the throttles back and called for cruise power. Then our attention was diverted to a brilliant orange glow low in the southeast sky. We thought it might be a distress flare. I called the center and reported what we had observed. If we had known at that time what we were witnessing, it would have made for a solemn evening. It wasn't until we were on the return trip late that night that we learned what we had witnessed.

That night in early April of 1961, two F-100s out of Kirtland Air Force Base in New Mexico tracked a B-52 bomber to make their simulated practice run. A Sidewinder missile suddenly bolted from one of the F-100s to sniff out the hot gasses from the B-52. There was an intense orange flash and smoke and the bomber began twisting crazily out of the night sky to impact the slopes of Mount Taylor in New Mexico. Five crewmen were able to bail out and survived the spiraling infernal, but were badly injured. Three others were unable to escape and went down with the bomber. What we had supposed to be a flare, several miles from our position, in reality was the appalling demise of a B-52 bomber 500 miles away. Later a board of inquiry revealed a tiny drop of moisture shorted out a circuit, releasing the Sidewinder to scent out the hot gasses from the B-52.

16

The Stew

The unusual camaraderie among DC-3 crews fostered some great times: some hilarious, some merely humorous, and some serious. Many of these experiences involved flight attendants. Enough cannot be said about the flight attendants who served with Frontier. Back then they were all young women and each one was known to the passengers as the stewardess; but among the flight crews each was known respectfully as "the stew." They were our public relations representatives to the passengers, and I would like to tell you a little of their duties.

The stew served as the sole cabin attendant aboard the DC-3, and on the stormiest nights when the Grand Ol' Lady was pitching and rolling in the elements, she walked a tightrope up and down the aisle faithfully attending to her passengers' needs. Those who regarded the stewardess as a glorified waitress only revealed how little they'd flown.

As the sole qualified attendant in a DC-3 cabin, the stew instructed the passengers for unplanned emergencies, such as how to open the main cabin airstairs and emergency window exits, and the proper procedure for exiting the aircraft in the event of a gear-up landing. She had to know proper procedures in case of an in-flight cabin fire and how to handle an incapacitated passenger. It was imperative that she be prepared for the many situations and/or emergencies that could occur. Although actual emergencies were rare, and most stews never had that experience, her dedication to the safety of her passengers was her first priority and she did it well.

The cabin duties consisted of making her passengers comfortable by passing out gum and offering pillows. Blankets were available if a cold cabin made it necessary, and it usually was. Along with consommé soup, coffee, tea, orange juice, and sometimes tomato juice were served; they were kept in large thermos bottles strapped to a rack in the companionway.

For several years after replacing the stewards on Challenger, the responsibility was passed on to the stew to enter into Compartment A to sort and rearrange the mail sacks in preparation for the next station. Entering the rear compartment she would look every bit the lady in her uniform, white gloves, and three-inch high heels. As soon as the door closed she would rip off the white gloves and stagger around in her high heels while throwing sacks of mail hither and thither. After this chore was completed she dusted off her hands, straightened her hair, pulled the white gloves back on and daintily stepped into the passenger cabin looking every bit the lady. In spite of all this, newly-hired stews were the target of many pranks by the pilots.

Retractable Tailwheel

This story has been handed down since the early fifties. How true it is I would hesitate to venture a guess. But they say it happened on Frontier and involved one of our veteran stews out of Billings, Montana, who has since passed on to that big hangar in the sky. One of our new-hire copilots, having heard of the tailwheel prank, decided to spring it on the stew. After takeoff in the DC-3, he notified her there seemed to be a problem with the tailwheel not retracting into the rear compartment

(DC–3 tailwheels do not retract). He asked if she would go back to the tail compartment and check to see if anything looked wrong.

She stepped out of the cockpit smiling to herself. After a short wait, she rubbed a little smudge on her hands and stepped back into the cockpit. She said, "Things didn't look right back there so I yanked on this long bolt; it slipped out and the tailwheel and its components fell to the earth."

The stunned copilot sat there with his mouth open until the captain and stewardess broke out laughing. The new hire hadn't realized he was flying with one of our veteran stews who knew her way around an airplane.

St. Elmo's Fire

Sometimes when flying in precipitation at night, we were privileged to watch the antics of St. Elmo's fire. This phenomena consists of a luminous bluish flame that dances and skips around the windshield. You could gently lay your hand next to the windshield, and the flame from outside the windshield would follow the path of your hand as you moved it about.

If a newly-hired stew should step into the cockpit to see this unusual manifestation for the first time, we had to quickly assure her it was a natural presentation exhibited by the master showperson, Mother Nature, and not of the supernatural.

Old sailing masters who saw St. Elmo's fire dancing in the rigging at the top of the mast took it as a good omen. Not wanting to be contrary, I espoused their belief.

17

Well You Have Now

Tink Thiese, maintenance supervisor, tells of the time he was riding jump seat (extra seat in cockpit) with Captain Al Mooney at the controls on a ferry flight to Utah without passengers:

> **Tink Thiese:** *Captain Mooney asked me if I had heard of a DC-3 doing a roll. I said I hadn't, and thought it to be impossible with this lumbering transport.*
>
> *Captain Mooney lowered the nose, and as I watched the airspeed build up, he pulled back on the yoke and rolled her into one of the smoothest rolls imaginable. It was like the earth was doing the rolling, and we were stationary—it was that smooth. Then Mooney commented, "Well, you have now."*

Captain Mooney was born into an aviation family. All of his brothers were associated with aviation. His dad, Captain Bert Mooney, was one of Western Airline's early pilots; for many years he served as chief pilot for Western's Salt Lake based crews. The airport at Butte, Montana was named Mooney Air Field in Bert Mooney's honor.

The Sampling Mechanic

Tink told about one mechanic who was always fiddling around under the DC-3:

> *There was a particular mechanic who if he saw a spot of liquid on a DC-3's exterior, he would sample it with his tongue to try to determine if it was fuel, oil, or hydraulic fluid. I knew I had to break the mechanic's habit of tasting everything in or on an airplane. The day would soon come when we would be flying upgraded equipment. This meant that hydraulic fluid would be the dangerous Skydrol, a fluid that was poisonous if ingested.*

Drastic steps had to be taken to break his obsession. One day, I knew the "sampling mechanic" would soon be coming on duty. With no one watching, I urinated on the wheel brake assembly. The sampling mechanic was soon making the rounds fiddling under the DC-3 and tasting all the damp spots.

Looking out the window of the mechanic's shack, I watched as he stopped and scrutinized the fluid dripping down the wheel assembly. The mechanic would think he had located a hydraulic leak, and I watched as he wiped a finger through the liquid and sampled it with his tongue. Too late! With his keen sense of taste he realized what he had just sampled. He rushed into the mechanic's shack spitting and sputtering, "Some damn dog let go on the DC-3, and if I find the SOB, I'll kill it." I thought long and hard on this, but decided it was best not to say anything. But I accomplished what I had set out to do: that "damn dog" broke the sampling mechanic of imbibing in airplane liquids.

A write-up in the aircraft maintenance book by the captain:

Right #2 window appears to have a four-inch crack in the outer pane.

Write-off by the mechanic in the maintenance book:

Inspected right #2 window. What appeared to be a four-inch crack, was the remains of a bug—removed bug remains.

18

Did We Do That?

One incident that still brings laughter involved flying over New Mexico in the summertime, which was not a piece of cake. On many of the short legs it was impractical to climb the DC-3 high enough over the tortured desert areas, that were hotter than Mexican chili, to avoid the superheated air. It was continuous turbulence for the entire flight and many of the passengers got airsick.

Back then, there was an empty malted milk carton placed in each seatback for the passengers' use. We called them burp cups. On this particular day Mother Nature had the furnace turned up with heat waves bouncing off the desert floor and mirages beckoning on the horizon. The turbulence was strutting its expertise, making the Grand Ol' Lady pay for treading through its domain. Our stewardess, Helen Etzel, was on the run, handing out airsick pills and getting rid of overflowing burp cups.

After we arrived in Albuquerque and all the passengers had deplaned, the cleaning agents came aboard, rolled up the soiled carpets and carried them off the aircraft in preparation for newly-laundered and deodorized carpets to be brought aboard. As I made my way to the rear exit, I saw Helen standing at the commissary pouring you-know-what from one burp cup to another.

I asked, "Helen! What are you doing?"

"Shhhh! See that sweet little old lady standing out there with the gray hair? She lost her teeth in one of these burp cups and I'm trying to find them."

I didn't stick around.

Helen has been retired for more years than we like to remember. She resides in Toledo, Ohio, and remembers this episode as though it were only yesterday.

Snakes Alive

There was one stewardess who must have been around when Orville and Wilbur first flew the Wright Flyer. She seldom came into the cockpit to offer refreshments, and when she did, she would stand there with a titter that sounded like a golf ball rolling into the cup.

One dark, moonless night when we thought she might be having difficulty staying awake in the rear of the aircraft, we contrived a fabrication to liven things up and keep her awake for the remainder of the night.

After flipping the companionway light switch off, I hit the stewardess call button and we waited for her to enter the dark cockpit. She served us a couple of cold beverages and I began to talk about our mythical payload in the cargo hold. I told her that we were transporting two large anacondas to the local zoo. That got her attention.

"You mean there are two large snakes right up here in the cargo area?"

"That's right," I answered. "They're up here where we can keep them warm."

"I hate snakes! They give me the creeps," she said. "They'd better be caged real good. I'm returning to the cabin as fast as I can." She hesitantly soft-shoed it through the dark.

Now was the time to put our plan into action. The DC-3 has a companionway between the cabin door and the cockpit. On either side is a storage area with a cargo-restraining net securing the cargo. The copilot hurried aft, unhooked one side of the restraining harness, slipped into the hold, and secured the harness.

I hit the stewardess call button. A few minutes later she slowly opened the door to reveal the dark passageway and cautiously placed one foot through the door. From his crouched position, the copilot reached out in the dark and grabbed her ankle. There was a momentary pause, and then she let go with an ear-piercing shriek. With one leap she disappeared into the cabin. When the copilot peeked through the door, he saw she had landed midway back in the cabin.

All the sleeping passengers bolted upright with panic in their eyes. The copilot slammed the cabin door and rushed back to his seat in the cockpit. His only words were, "Captain Searle, we may be in trouble!" She never returned to the cockpit during that flight, and we never heard how she explained her behavior to the passengers. After we had blocked in and were in the process of checking out, I innocently asked, "What was going on back there?" With a voice that resembled a typewriter in slow motion, she shook her head with a vacant expression, and ambled on, "I'm not sure what happened, but I thought a snake had me. I guess I was just imagining it."

The copilot and I thought it best to let her *just imagine*. With all the commotion she created, and scaring the wits out of the passengers (and me), it was better just to forget it, and that's what I did. Until now.

Expedited Bus Service

CAPTAIN MATT FERGUSON AND CAPTAIN TEX SEARLE

In those days it was the stewardess's responsibility to carry her own commissary kit, a small suitcase-type bag filled with instant soup, coffee, tea, airsick pills, and lots of Doublemint chewing gum to help the passengers relieve the pressure in their ears from the constant pressure changes of flying in unpressurized equipment.

On this occasion, as we prepared to board our flight at Riverton, Wyoming, Captain Matt Furguson noticed our stew's commissary kit still sitting by the boarding gate. He asked an agent to slip it in the rear cargo compartment without drawing the attention of the stew. After departure the stew rushed into the cockpit, and in a distraught voice informed us she had left her kit at the boarding gate.

Captain Ferguson reassuringly told her not to fret, that we would radio back to Riverton and have the commissary kit forwarded to Rock Springs by bus so it would be waiting there upon our arrival.

After the stew left the cockpit, I was asked to call ahead to Rock Springs and advise the agent that our stew's commissary kit was in the rear cargo compartment. On our arrival he was to remove it from the cargo compartment, open the main airstair door, hand it to our stewardess, and tell her a bus had brought it down from Riverton.

At Rock Springs everything proceeded as planned. Handing the kit to the relieved stewardess, the agent carried the prank further by advising her that a cab had been hired to carry her kit to the airport from the bus station, and there would be a $2.00 charge for the cab fare. She thanked him for his trouble and, not having the $2.00 with her, said she would co-mail (company mail) it to him.

Two days later when I was back in Rock Springs, the agent stepped into the cockpit with a smile on his face and asked, "What am I to do with this?" In his hand was the $2.00 the stew had promised and a note thanking him again for his trouble.

But this wasn't the end. Several days later, the stew was again in Riverton and the agent there who had slipped her kit in the rear cargo compartment told her that she owed him $2.00. She yelled, "You think I'm stupid? I've already paid $2.00 to the agent in Rock Springs. Why do I have to pay you?"

He explained that the bus firm had charged him $2.00 to carry the kit to Rock Springs for her to pick up there. She said, "Oh, I forgot about the bus."

All the money she had divvied over was returned to her via co-mail, and to my knowledge, no one ever did have the courage to tell her it was all a prank and that airplanes have managed to outrun ground transportation vehicles since 1903.

19

Steam Boiler Operators

Captain George L. Sims, now retired and living in Phoenix, Arizona had many interesting experiences while flying during his career. He has reached back in time to the day he and Captain Rich stoked boilers on DC-3s:

Captain George Sims: *Flying the Gooney Bird was a privilege. When I think back to all the aircraft I've flown, the Grand Ol' Lady stands above them all. You really flew that airplane; it was a completely hand-flown airplane. "Needle, ball, and airspeed"—at least that's what they used to holler all the time. You usually wound up going down faster than you went up. I remember one incident in the winter of 1948 when I was flying for Challenger Airlines on the run from Salt Lake City to Denver, Colorado; Bob Rich was my copilot.*

Challenger was expanding her routes, and, needing more equipment, had leased a DC-3 from Continental Air Lines. It was a nice airplane. It had a good heating system: one of the old flash-type boilers that was located in the exhaust stack of the right-hand engine and a steam radiator located under the floor of the cargo compartment at the forward section of the airplane. It had all the necessary valves and ducts plumbed throughout the aircraft for steam heating that not only heated the interior of the aircraft, but also furnished needed heat to the windshield for the prevention of ice accumulation.

In cold weather operations, it was extremely important that the cold air nose valve in the ventilating system never be opened wide enough to cause the steam pressure to drop below 5 pounds. With the pressure below 5 pounds there was a good chance of a system freeze-up. Altitude also affected the steam pressure: the higher we flew, the less dense the air, causing lower steam pressure. On the ground with the right engine shut down, we had to follow certain guidelines to prevent a freeze-up by draining the system. It was only as good as the pilot operating it, so besides being pilots we were also steam boiler operators.

After passing over Cheyenne, we started planning for the Adcock Low Frequency Range approach into Denver. The weather report was a 500-foot ceiling with freezing temperatures on the ground. The maintenance people had demanded, "Be damn sure you turn the heat off before landing, so as not to have a boiler freeze up on the ground." In the vicinity of Greeley, Colorado, I thought about the boiler and asked Bob Rich to please turn it off. He promptly did.

Letting down in preparation for landing, I'm sure that I acted too soon in shutting the boiler down. The windshield iced over and it was as if someone had pulled down the blinds. We then pulled up and cleared the area. Bob and I looked at each other and said "to hell with it." We cranked the boiler back into operation and got it twice as hot for the next approach which turned out okay. It did not freeze after landing. Nice airplane.

Author's note: The weight and balance of a C-47 (DC-3) was only as good as the cargo-master, or the person in charge of loading. Many times during the early years of WWII the C-47 was called upon to operate in-and-out of dirt or gravel strips that often were moisture sodden. Often over grossed as much as 5,000 pounds, and the weight and balance nowhere near the in-limits, the antics of the C-47 struggling to become airborne reminded one of the huge gooney bird, a seabird from the Pacific Islands. The name has become a part of the DC-3 legacy.

There are many stories of the Gooney Bird's lifting capacity. Originally the DC-3 was designed as a twenty-one passenger aircraft. In WWII the C-47 was helping to carry out the evacuation of Burma, and among her seventy-four passengers was Lt. Col. Jimmy Doolittle who was returning from a bombing raid over Tokyo. In Vietnam, the C-47 has been credited with carrying over 100 refugees, many of whom were children that were crammed into her interior.

In addition to the 10,000-plus DC-3s constructed in the United States, it is estimated there were another 2,000-plus built in Russia under license as the Lisunow Li-2, and an additional 500-odd in Japan known as "tabby" by the Allies in the Pacific theatre of operations.[9]

20

High Altitude Humor

Captain Chick Stevens: *High altitude and inflatable boobs don't mix. After leaving Pueblo, Colorado, en route to Durango, it is a max climb exertion all the way to Walsenburg intersection for the DC-3 to reach an altitude that would safely traverse the backbone of the Sangre De Cristo Mountains. With lofty peaks well over 14,000 feet, La Veta Pass along with Monarch Pass are two of the highest passes in the United States the DC-3s had to ascend.*

Crews still laugh about the time the DC-3 was climbing to 11,000 feet to make its way through La Veta pass. The stewardess noticed a lady passenger struggling in her seat. She stopped to ask if she could be of help, but the problem was staring her in the face. She ran into the cockpit and explained to me, "I've got a real problem in the cabin—would you come back?" When I rushed back to see what the problem was, it was staring me in the face as well. A distressed woman was trying to conceal two overly-expanded enhancers under a severely stretched blouse with buttons that were ready to fly on their own.

Flying in the high, thin air, the compressed air in the inflatable bra had expanded to such an immense volume, making this struggling passenger the most overly-endowed individual that the stewardess or I had ever laid eyes on. I rushed back to the cockpit and leveled the DC-3 off so as not to expand the problem any further. After leveling off at 11,000 feet the inflatable cheaters ceased expanding. We prevented an onboard catastrophe by stopping the notable assets from blowing up in her face. With hardly a word of thanks, the embarrassed lady kept a vigilant watch out the window, and wondered why we were flying so low through the pass.

Late Breakfast

As the DC-3 descended out of the night sky and settled onto the tarmac at Rochester, New York, the weary crew felt the tires of the DC-3 spin their greeting to the runway. The military charter had been a long haul from San Antonio, Texas with two stops thrown in for fuel. With the amount of time it would take to fly the charter, the company had crewed the DC-3 with two captains. Ed Walker would be the acting #1 captain with Chick Stevens as #2, and Warren Heckman would be serving as copilot. There would be no stew aboard.

They put the DC-3 to roost as quickly as possible to save time for the short layover the trip called for. They looked at their watches and saw it was 2:00 a.m. The schedule called for a departure that morning at 10:00 with twenty-four GIs bound for Cheyenne, Wyoming. The ground transportation was late arriving to take them to the hotel. The ride was long and would cut into their rest. When checking in at the hotel, the flight deck crew found they would all be billeted in the same room with a partition that had two beds on one side and one on the other. They requested a wake-up call and turned in.

Warren Heckman answered the phone for the wake-up call after only a short rest. He quickly showered and shaved to give the two captains on the other side of the partition more time to sleep. When Heckman finished he woke the other two crewmembers and asked if they planned on flying that day. Waiting on each other to shave and shower took longer than they had planned, and with the long ride to the airport they were running late so had to skip breakfast.

Without breakfast, Captain Ed Walker could turn into a mean biting bear, and soon did. After the twenty-four military personnel were aboard, strapped down, and the doors secured, Captain Ed Walker started the engines without calling for any assistance from the copilot. When they received their routing clearance over the radio, it was a different than what they had requested. This seemed to upset the temperament of the #1 captain even more. As they taxied to the runway, Captain Chick Stevens, who was occupying the copilot seat, reached for the microphone to request takeoff clearance. He soon discovered that all was not well, and that all he'd be required to do was to manage the cowl flaps.

Without calling for the checklist, Captain Walker read it to himself and then marked off the necessary items one by one. Keying the mike button he called for takeoff clearance. After lift off and the gear shocks had extended, the toebrakes were softly applied to halt the spinning rotation of the wheels before they tucked into their wells. The expected call never came for the gear up request. Exercising his captain authority, Walker leaned down and unlatched the gear safety-latch handle, pulled it up, and raised the gear handle leaving acting copilot Stevens with few duties to carry out.

The DC-3 skirted Lake Erie as it continued its long 1,450 mile flight to Cheyenne with planned fuel stops at Detroit and North Platte, Nebraska. The mood in the cockpit was dismal with no dialogue between the crewmembers. Sitting on the jumpseat Warren Heckman decided the atmosphere in the cockpit needed changing, and the only way to do this was by grubbing up a few victuals for the #1 captain. But this was a bare-cupboard run, and there was no food service aboard.

Copilot Heckman walked back to the commissary and found a paper plate and cup. He proceeded to rip up scraps of paper into little strips and bunched them into a small pile on the paper plate. He wrote "ham and eggs" on a note and laid it on the scraps of paper. On another he wrote "hot cakes." Then he wrote "toast and jelly" on paper the size of a slice of bread, and on a paper cup filled with water he scribbled "coffee." Carrying the paper plate in one hand and the paper cup in another, he returned to the cockpit and tapped Captain Walker on the shoulder and said, "Breakfast is served."

When Captain Chick Stevens, who was performing the copilot duties, saw what was going on he cringed in his seat—he knew the cork was about to blow and the whole airplane was going to explode. Captain Walker turned to see who was tapping him on the shoulder. Remembering this moment as though it were yesterday, Captain Chick Stevens said, "I couldn't bear to watch what my friend had brought on himself or maybe on both of us. I watched as Captain Walker looked at the paper plate, his neck turning red. He looked up at Heckman and then at the paper plate again. Even the sound of the engines on the Grand Ol' Lady seemed to shrink to a whisper waiting for the inevitable to happen.

"But it didn't happen! Instead, Ed Walker broke into a grin that Warren and I still remember. The noonday sun lit up the cockpit with bright sunbeams, the engines of the Grand Ol' Lady returned to their robust sound that all is well, and as I looked at a smiling Warren Heckman and he looked at me—there just wasn't anything we could say. The continuation of that trip was a piece of cake."

Captain Stevens was made Supervisor of Flight Training in 1959. He was given authority to select three captains from the line to assist him. All pilots in the Flight Training Department would be called FAA designated check airman. Captain Stevens would be in charge of all flight and pilot ground-school training, including new hires, captain and copilot proficiency checks, instructing in the simulators, and writing new aircraft flight manuals.

Captain Stevens visited the training departments of many of the major carriers, and from the different procedures he observed, he selected the most significant, incorporated them into a standardized procedure, and from this came the stabilized approach. This makes for a much safer and better crew coordination in the cockpit in knowing ahead of time what to expect of each other and to what configuration the airplane will be in and when. Crews now would configure the airplane to prescribed procedures as called for in the training manual. Crews were trained to make certain altitude callouts when approaching assigned altitudes, and also both altitude and speed callouts during visual and instrument approaches.

Before starting an approach the crews made positive checks of the two altimeters for being in limits. On a low approach the one not flying would call 1,000 feet above the touchdown elevation, and then call 50 feet above the minimum descent altitude to alert the pilot flying that he either has 50 feet to break out of the weather and land, or that he should prepare to change from a landing configuration to a climb configuration, and climb for the safety of the sky. The FAA highly approved of these procedures and many airlines incorporated them into their own training programs.

The FAA notified all scheduled airlines they would be required to write a flight training manual and submit it to the FAA Washington office for approval by July 1, 1960. The flight manual written by Captain Chick Stevens was the first to be accepted.

A Chicken Doing 450 Miles Per Hour

Captain Stevens remembers one ground school class in particular:

I'll never forget one of the first ground school classes I taught. The subject was the new bird-proof windshields on the jets. In the old days, windshields on propeller-driven aircraft were not much stronger than those on automobiles. A two- to five-pound bird hitting a windshield at 200 mph or so would go right through the windshield. Many pilots in those days were seriously injured from bird strikes.

I played a movie for the class that covered the new bird-proof windshields. A segment showed dead chickens being fired at the windshield with a special gun. I said, "There you are, guys, a ten-pound chicken hitting the glass at 450 mph."

Some clown in the back raised his hand and asked, "May I assume sir, that the windshield would also withstand the impact of a 450-pound chicken going ten mph?"

Captain Chick Stevens served six years in the Army Air Corps. During WWII he flew the hump in the Curtiss built C-46 Commando. He was also the editor of the popular *Frontier Magazine*. After 28,000 hours plus, and a thirty-year career with Frontier Airlines, his flying career was cut short by a medical disability at the young age of fifty-five. Captain Stevens resides in Aurora, Colorado.

Captain Ed Walker served in the U.S. Navy in WWII and flew the R4D/DC-3. He passed away in the late 1960s.

Captain Warren Heckman learned to fly in 1939 in the Civilian Pilot Training program at Laramie, Wyoming, called the Plains Airways School. It was one of three schools owned by Pic Walker, the late father of Captain Billy Walker. In May of 1950, Captain Heckmen hired on with Monarch Airlines, shortly before the merger with Challenger and Arizona Airways. After a career of almost thirty-one years flying the mountain empire and experiencing the growth of Frontier as it spread its wings over the U.S., Canada, and Mexico, Captain Heckman retired from Frontier in December of 1980 per the FAA mandatory retirement age of 60 years.

Not ready for the rocking chair, Captain Heckman hired on with American Airlines as a ground school and simulator instructor. He continued this course for 6-½ years, then, continued on with America West airlines in their training program for another eight years. After being associated with aviation for forty-six years, including 32,000-plus hours spent in the cockpits of a multitude of aircraft, Captain Heckman turned in the key to the cockpit in 1995. He resides in Scottsdale, Arizona.

21

Twenty-Three Sick Marines

Captain Dick Adair started pushing throttles for Frontier in 1949. He began his thirty-two year career flying DC-3s over the Rocky Mountain empire and ended it manipulating thrust levers on high-flying jets over the continental U.S., Mexico, and Canada.

Captain Adair, better known as Captain Wyley, a name Challenger pilots bestowed upon him in 1949, relates that as a youth his early interest in airplanes kept him busy peddling his bike several miles to the Salt Lake City Airport to watch the aircraft:

Captain "Wyley": *The one plane that drew my attention was the new DC-3. It was love at first sight. In the 1930s money was hard to come by, but in 1939 I had put enough money aside to take my first ride in a Piper Cub. From that moment on I was addicted to flying, and I knew it would be my life's work.*

On July 28, 1943, I soloed my first airplane in Salt Lake City. Shortly after, I moved to San Diego to continue my schooling and received my commercial and instrument ratings as well as the instructor rating, and continued on to receive the airline transport rating. Before long I was flying for San Diego Sky Freight. They had acquired two C-47s that were converted into DC-3s and were kept busy flying military personnel throughout the United States.

Flying with ex-military pilots who had not as yet received their civilian instrument tickets, I had to fill out all the flight plans and sign the releases. One time, while flying a charter from Kansas City to Phoenix, Arizona, the Grand Ol' Lady was churning up the air when, in the vicinity of Winslow, Arizona, we picked up turbulence as we worked our way through a line of thunderstorms. The twenty-three Marines aboard were already feeling a little nervous when the plane was suddenly thrown violently onto its back. After this occurrence, they all became sick and wanted to surrender to mother earth. From this lesson I always tried to give a wide path to Mother Nature—can you imagine what twenty-three airsick Marines can do to the interior of a DC-3?

In August of 1949, Wyley made his first copilot trip for Challenger Airlines.

Airframe Icing

I look back with pride to those early years of flying the DC-3 and experiencing the camaraderie of my fellow pilots as we hauled mail throughout the Rocky Mountains. At that time, no other airplane could have accomplished what the DC-3 was called upon to do. The punishment this airplane endured in the turbulence thrown at her by the unstable air over the Rockies was unbelievable. The many landings were an everyday chore for her. The engines had to endure almost as much time in climb power as they normally would in cruise power, and yes, they spent a great deal of time grinding out max power. The confidence we had in those engines on black nights over such rugged terrain brought great peace. Not only were the engines steady and sound, but we knew we had the top radial engine mechanics in the business.

While returning to Salt Lake City, we were over Huntsville, Utah, a small town nestled in the canyons of the Wasatch Range, we began to accumulate the expected moderate ice. While flying over mountainous terrain in wintertime we endured three things: We expected to accrue heavy ice over the mountains, we couldn't let down to a warmer temperature because of the high terrain, and we couldn't climb higher because we were already there.

Packing a moderate load of ice on the airframe, we arrived over Ogden, Utah and banked left to commence our letdown into the Salt Lake Valley when we felt and heard a terrific chatter on the fuselage above our heads. I looked at Captain Mooney and he looked at me. Then we heard a strange noise, and a red flag appeared indicating our VHF NAV was INOP. We quickly switched from a VOR approach to an ADF approach and continued letting down out of the ice into Salt Lake City.

On the ground an inspection was performed to determine the mystery. Our suspicions were confirmed when the mechanics discovered the VHF NAV antenna had become so heavy and unbalanced from encrusted ice buildup that it had sheared off leaving a gaping hole in the top of the DC-3.

Wild Chicks

The agents at the Denver station had loaded a half dozen cardboard boxes filled with baby chicks in the forward cargo hold to keep them warm during their transport to Phoenix. Glen Gettman was my copilot, and we had commenced our let-down into the Phoenix area when we heard chirping that was becoming louder. Looking down we discovered a brood of baby chicks running around on the deck and under our seats. They had escaped from a damaged box. About this time the stew opened the door to enter, and many of the baby chicks took off down the aisle between the passenger seats. The passengers were good-natured about it, and after we landed they helped us gather the chicks and place them back in the box.

Wyley's One-Engine Stop

One time during the early 1950s, I was sweet-talking the Grand Ol' Lady through heavy weather en route to Riverton, Wyoming with a planned stop at Rock Springs. The Rock Springs station reported a moderate snowstorm in progress at the airport. Falling and blowing snow were wreaking havoc on the runway and visibility was below landing minimums. I let down to 10,000 feet, the minimum enroute altitude to Rock Springs. If visibility improved, I would be in a position to execute an immediate approach.

While flying over Rock Springs, the latest weather report gave us minimums for landing with a reported six inches of powdered snow on the runway. We flew the instrument approach to runway 25, and after rolling out to the west end of the runway, we reversed course to make the long taxi east to the terminal. The feathery snow was still swirling on the runway from the prop blast and gusty surface winds, so I elected to hold a moment until visibility improved.

The stewardess, thinking this was a one-engine stop and that we had arrived at the terminal, released the airstair door and let the several passengers deplane. With help from an onboard passenger, she pulled the airstair door back up and latched it to prevent the swirling snow from entering the aircraft. When I saw the door warning light come on, I crawled out of the seat and proceeded to the cabin to investigate. As I stepped into the cabin, I saw that the airstair was closed and the passengers were seated, so I returned to the cockpit. The warning light had gone out indicating the airstair door was safely closed. With the runway visibility picking up, we proceeded to make the long taxi to the terminal where I intended to investigate the door warning problem.

The stewardess, thinking the Rock Springs agent hadn't had time to board the weight manifest, immediately rushed to the cockpit to inform me the manifest was not on board. I asked, "What manifest? We haven't even arrived at the terminal yet."

The DC-3 returned to the far west boundary of the airport where we located the bewildered passengers all huddled together in the wind-driven snow. After the passengers were enplaned for the second time, they were safely transported to the Rock Springs Terminal. Most airlines charge passengers for an additional stop, but not this time.

Wyley's Bushy Red Tail

I remember receiving an unexpected trophy from one flight. We had just touched down at Casper, Wyoming, when a red fox darted into the DC-3's path. The company radio informed me that we had assassinated a red fox. I mentioned I would sure like to have that red tail. On my return flight they presented me with the red tail and I tied it to my jeep antenna. The bushy red tail was quite a conversation piece.

Captain Wyley reminds us of the foxes, deer, antelope, coyotes, and sage hens whose sad fate it was to become entangled in the propellers of a swift-moving aircraft on the runway. These incidents seldom occurred, but when they did, it usually happened at night when all the crew could make out were the eyes of the darting victims as they reflected the glare of the landing lights. It was a desperate feeling as there was little the crews could do to avoid these sickening tragedies at remote airports.

Captain Wyley says that every time he flew into Wyoming in the winter, he expected to meet a cold front pushing through the state accompanied by high gusty winds:

Ice Covered Ramps

At Cheyenne in winter months, we had to take extra precautionary measures to prevent the DC-3 from being blown sideways off the ice-covered ramp. The passengers were warned that when walking on the icy ramp and leaning into the gusty wind, should it suddenly die they were in danger of pitching forward on their face (or something else if the wind was to their backs).

One Wyoming resident told me of a rooster in the Southpass area that had leaned down to peep into a beer bottle, and found itself imprisoned in the bottle from the force of the wind. To back me up on these tales, Chief Pilot Scott Keller remembers flying over Sherman Hill to Laramie and he couldn't keep up with the westbound cars and trucks on the old Lincoln highway from the force of the high westerly winds.

My Brother

Something pleasant happened to me a long time ago that I won't forget. While flying my trip from Albuquerque, New Mexico to El Paso, Texas with a stop at Alamogordo, New Mexico I was eastbound about thirty miles out of Albuquerque enjoying the landscape from 2,000 feet. On the company frequency, I heard a voice call, "Hey Wyley!" I thought it might be the station calling. I asked, "Who is this?" The voice answered, "It's your brother Mark." What a nice surprise. I asked him his location. He answered, "I'm inbound from the east following Highway 66 into Albuquerque about forty-five miles out." He was on one of his first trips flying captain on a DC-3 for Continental Airlines. A couple of minutes later we spotted each other, and flashed our landing lights in recognition. He said, "I never thought I'd see the day we would cross paths in DC-3s in the middle of nowhere." We opened our sliding side windows and waved as we passed. I had taught Mark to fly years ago, and it was a great experience to see my younger brother flying as a new captain. He went on to fly the Pacific when Continental had the MATs contract for flying the military and he also served as the chief pilot in Los Angeles.

Wyley's Missed Trip

While the DC-3 was still parked at the Kansas City Airport ramp, I slipped aboard and into the cockpit without drawing the stew's attention. When the copilot came aboard he advised the stew that as I hadn't made my appearance yet, and if I was not aboard when they buttoned up to let him know. She handed the copilot the manifest and assured him she would watch for the captain. A short time later the airstair door was closed and latched, and the stewardess's attention was drawn to the passengers.

We taxied out to the runway and after the checklist was completed, we took off. A short time later, after departing the traffic area, I slipped out of my seat and entered the forward cargo hold. The copilot then summoned the stewardess to the cockpit and asked her where the captain was. Panic-stricken, she explained that she had forgotten to watch for the captain after becoming occupied with the passengers. The copilot, looking concerned, suggested they continue on to Omaha and not say anything about their problem to the passengers. He would try to bluff this out somehow so they wouldn't be in trouble.

After the stew's departure from the cockpit, I stepped from the cargo hold and returned to my duties in the cockpit. Upon our arrival at Omaha, the station agents, who were in on the hoax, quickly pushed the conveyer up to the hamburger door that was located just aft of the cockpit abeam the large propellers, and I hurried down it. When the agent dropped the airstairs, the stewardess looked out. She became flustered when she saw me at the foot of the airstairs wiping my brow and looking exhausted. When I boarded the aircraft I complained to the aghast stewardess, "I never had to run so fast in my life, thanks to you."

This story has been widely circulated through the generations and retold many times, but it really happened to Wyley. Now in his retirement years, Captain Wyley resides in Colorado and reminisces about the golden years of flying.

22

That Lying Passenger

Captain Al Kendell tells of a time they were climbing out of Hastings, Nebraska in a DC-3. In the distance you could see the large Navy arsenal where munitions were stored in uniform rows of underground facilities covered with mounds of earth.

Captain Al Kendell: *The stew entered the cockpit and asked, "What are those large mounds we can see?" Feeling in a jesting mood, I told her they were Indian burial mounds.*

She blurted out, "That lying passenger in the cabin told me they were arsenals."

Memoirs of the Ceiling

Cruising at 13,000 feet, Captain Kendell could do nothing but shake his head when the stew told him of her latest episode in the cabin of the DC-3:

I was walking up the aisle and I felt a tug on my skirt. I turned and a small, elderly lady motioned me to lean down so she could whisper to me. She asked where the bathroom was. I told her to follow me and I would lead the way. At the rear of the aircraft, I held the door open until she was inside the blue room. I walked to the forward section of the cabin and when I turned around I was stunned to see she was back in her seat again. She wasn't in the blue room thirty seconds, and there she sat, motioning me to come to her. She whispered, "I need a newspaper." A gentleman in the next seat offered his paper and said he was finished with it.

Once again she returned to the blue room. I surmised that she liked to read while sitting on the john. After a lengthy period of time, I began to worry about her, but she finally reappeared and returned to her seat. This series of events was eating on my mind, and I couldn't figure it out. I noticed she'd forgotten her newspaper so I stepped back to the blue room to retrieve it. You're not going to believe this, but she had stuck the newspaper all over the overhead of the blue room. She wet it with water and plastered it on good. I'd never run into a situation like this before so had to know what was going on. I paused by her seat and asked why the newspaper was stuck on the blue room overhead. She whispered, "When I started to use the bathroom, I looked up and saw the little window in the ceiling. Well, I didn't want anybody up there peeking down at me and watching, so I fixed it."

Short Notice

There is another story that remains in Captain Al Kendell's memory files. He was at the controls of a Propjet 580 when the stew entered the cockpit and asked him if he had a key to the blue room because the door would not open. "There is a lady back there on short notice about to charge the blue room door," she said.

I told her the blue room door could only be locked from inside and requested that she take her seat until after we skirted a fast-approaching thunderstorm. The turbulence was already starting to build.

The stew blurted, "There's no one inside that blue room, but the door will not open. I'll have to try other means," and rushed from the cockpit.

A short time later the stew again entered the cockpit. This time she was wiping her arms and hands with paper towels as she informed me this would be her last trip. "As soon as we block in," she said, "I'm handing in my resignation. When I stepped out of the cockpit a woman demanded, 'I've got to pee, and I've got to pee now.' So I hurried her into the commissary and pulled the curtains. I emptied the ice bucket and told her to have at it. The turbulence was so bad she asked me to steady it while she tried to sit on it. Well, there we were, both sliding around on the floor, me trying to keep that bucket under her, and her missing the bucket and peeing on the floor and on me too. What time do we get on the ground?"

Ball Lightning

Captain Al Kendell tells about the time he and Captain Al Mooney were flying in obscured conditions when a brilliant, bluish ball of lightning appeared at the wingtip. "It grew until it was the size of a basketball. From the wing tip it rolled towards us and entered the cabin. It continued across the aisle and exited out the other side, then danced to the end of the wingtip where it disappeared. At the completion of the trip, we filed off the aircraft with trepidation," Kendell reported.

There are other stories that tell of ball lightning actually rolling down the aisle between startled passengers who sit frozen in their seats. Looking the other way, some try to ignore it hoping it will vanish. With high-performance aircraft now able to fly above the weather, we don't see so much of this unusual phenomenon.

I was piloting a Convair 340 at 17,000 feet over the southern Colorado Rockies in obscured weather. It was near midnight, and the copilot was fretting about the glow of light reflecting from the aircraft nose cone. As it continued to enlarge and grow brighter, he became quite vexed and demanded to know what the hell was going on out there.

I'd seen this strange phenomenon before, and it does present a hostile feeling to the old posterior; but before I could explain, the damn thing exploded. I thought I was going to lose a good copilot. From what I understand, ball lightning is a rare type of lightning shaped like a globe of fire. It usually disappears without a detonation, but has been known to burn holes in aircraft. In this case it let go with a vengeance that lightened up a dull trip with the smell of ozone filling the aircraft. It did not cause damage.

But my wife, Esther, saw it in our own home. She was alone in our family room one evening, feeling rather cozy as she listened to the thunder outside. Terrified, she watched ball lightning suddenly enter from the fireplace. It danced across the room to a window and made its exit. I can imagine her reaction, but regardless, she was a lot nicer to me after witnessing this phenomenon herself.

23

The Mad Scientist

Captain Seymour Isaacs had located a pair of eyeglasses with special one-half-inch thick lenses at a novelty store. When he put them on, he looked like the mad scientist who was in the terminal stage of blindness. When the urge hit him at the end of a trip, he'd slip them on and then walk close behind the copilot through the waiting area of the terminal. The passengers, waiting for their departure would casually look in the captain's direction when they noticed others nervously staring at him. They quickly straightened up in their seats, not believing what they were seeing, as this poor blind captain closely followed his copilot through the terminal.

Captain Isaacs enlisted in the Army Air Corps in September 1942. He attended Civil Service Aircraft Mechanical School and the School of Aeronautics. While waiting for a call to active duty, he was employed as an aircraft mechanic at the Rome Air Depot in Rome, New York. He was called to active duty for pilot training in February 1943. He was commissioned a second lieutenant, and after completing B-17 training he was assigned a crew and a B-17 which he transported over the water to England from the U.S. Often they returned to base after sustaining hits from fighters or shrapnel damage from German 88 anti-aircraft fire. Captain Isaacs shares the following experiences:

On one mission, the flak from anti-aircraft cannon bounced the planes around the sky like yo-yos. The tail gunner lost his composure and had to be restrained. On another mission, we took a hit in the bomb bay area that disabled my top turret gunner and ruptured our oxygen supply. Void of the primary oxygen supply, and with the B-17 badly damaged and unable to hold altitude, we had to leave the formation and drop to a lower altitude where the crew could breathe without supplemental oxygen. We had to return to the base alone, detached from the main bomb group. We felt fortunate to arrive safely as Me-109s and FW-190s were always on the prowl for wounded stragglers.

After flying thirty-three missions, I was rotated back stateside where I was trained to fly the B-24 Liberator, and the cargo version of the B-24 designated the C-87. The C-87 was also known as the Liberator Express. They were both manufactured by Consolidated Vultee. The C-82 Packet and the C-119 Flying Boxcar I flew were both manufactured by the Fairchild Company. The C-119 was an improved version of the Packet, and had the large Wright turbo compound engines. The crews liked to call it the high-handled wheelbarrow which it resembled. I was sent to South Carolina for my check out on the C-54 (civilian DC-4).

I served in the Military Air Transport with duty in Canada and the Arctic. Relieved of active duty in 1950, I began flying for Frontier Airlines. I was recalled to active duty in 1952 and served in Newfoundland. After being relieved from active duty again in 1955, I returned to Frontier. During my employment with Frontier, I also served in the Air Force Reserve, and then transferred to the Utah Air Guard. I retired from the Guard in 1967 and from Frontier in January 1984.

Reminiscence of the Blue Pacific

In November 1946, I was called to fly the C-54E (passenger configuration) to Hawaii. Departure was at night from what is now known as Travis Air Force Base. The flight plan called for a two-hour fuel reserve with no alternate specified for Hickam Field. Mild weather was forecast for the first half of the flight, but we soon encountered heavy weather after leaving the coast behind. Unable to navigate by celestial navigation, we expected—at the midway point—to receive a reliable fix from the Coast Guard ship on station: Ocean Station November. Voice and code communication were very poor. With the heavy weather prevailing, the Coast Guard departed their station and got underway to calmer seas north of the Pacific track where they could not offer a useable fix. The only option was dead reckoning—a method of flying compass headings and estimating distances traveled. Not a good situation in the middle of an ocean.

The radio operator stayed busy by trying to establish a reliable contact to relay our deteriorating circumstances. Flying in moderate turbulence with a passenger configuration of military and civilian personnel aboard was taxing the latrines to the limit. Changing altitudes in an attempt to locate smoother air was an exercise in futility. After about eight hours the weather abated somewhat and daylight broke through the clouds.

Using his best celestial capability, the navigator was able to take a couple of quick shots through breaks in the clouds. He determined we were more than eighty miles south of track because of the strong winds we had bucked. With this news came the realization we would not be able to make Hawaii even with our two-hour fuel reserve. The radio operator immediately broadcast a Mayday, gave our position and fuel on board, and then we operated under the extreme fuel management program.

Several hours after broadcasting the Mayday call, contact was established with an Air Sea Rescue B-17. The B-17 was fully equipped with a lifeboat suspended under its belly. With the B-17 trailing behind, we began a gradual rate of descent to conserve fuel while maintaining our present heading to the islands.

The previous year I had flown a C-47 to the airstrip on the island of Molokai and could vaguely remember it was located in the middle of the small island. After checking our charts we found the strip was now closed and had been deleted from all the charts. Since Molokai was located southeast of Oahu and situated on our present course, it was thought we might have a chance. After a discussion with the crew, the consensus was to attempt to reach the strip, or, if the tanks ran dry first, to dead-stick the C-54 onto the ocean.

Preparation and briefing the passengers for the ditching was completed, and a makeshift form of shoulder harnesses were rigged for my copilot and me from the extra cargo tie downs. Blankets were to be rolled up and laid on our laps to protect us from the whipping motion of the control column that sometimes occurs in ditching.

Eventually Molokai came over the horizon. All the fuel gauges were indicating empty. All the fuel tank selectors were selected ON, everything was cross-feed and the fuel boost pumps were positioned ON. It seemed like an eternity before we approached the island. I kept the C-54 a little high as the highest terrain was on our flight path to the strip. Both outboard engines failed and started to windmill. I had to make the decision now to either ditch in the ocean or go for it. The short strip was in sight, clear of obstacles and the altitude looked good.

Of the two alternatives, the strip looked more inviting, so it was a go. A right turn and number one, two, and four engines were all windmilling. A left turn to final with some crude slipping put us into a steep power-off descent. The fuel was gone, speed was fast at 140 mph, but we were home free. Why I didn't feather the outboards, I don't know. I probably didn't have time, or maybe I thought they would offer some wind resistance to help reduce my speed in the steep descent. As the tires made contact with the runway, I spiked it on and got on the brakes. The windmilling props provided hydraulic power for brakes and nose steering. You could hear the tires blow. The skid marks measured about 1,500 feet, and we were able to keep the aircraft on the small strip.

We radioed the B-17 overhead to inform them we were all okay. They relayed to Hickam that we were down and safe. A C-47 was dispatched loaded with drums of fuel, replacement wheels, and a maintenance crew to put the C-54 back in flying condition. Later, the maintenance crew sent word they found enough fuel from a fuel sump drain to fill a Zippo lighter. The fuel load programmed for the overwater leg was flight planned for eleven hours and twenty minutes en route plus two hours of reserve fuel. The actual flight lasted fourteen hours and forty minutes. Usually when an incident such as this occurs, a board of inquiry would be on your neck in a hurry. I never heard a word.

The DEW Line

In the early 1950s I was chief pilot over a squadron of C-54 aircraft built by the Douglas Aircraft Company, and C-119 aircraft built by the Fairchild Company. We were operating out of Stephenville, Newfoundland for the Northeast Air Command. Our flying assignments called for us to fly over the North Atlantic, Canada, Greenland, and the North Pole delivering cargo and personnel for the DEW (Distant Early Warning) line project. Much of the cargo was delivered by airdrops from the C-119 Fairchild. They had large clam doors that opened up at the rear of the aircraft for easy unloading of cargo from the air.

There were two drawbacks to using the C-119 with its 3,500-hp Wright Cyclone turbo compound engines. We had a series of engine failures, and at max gross the Fairchild would not hold altitude on a single engine. A call for help brought personnel from the Air Force, the Wright Cyclone Engine Company, and the Fairchild Aircraft Company.

Near the end of our review, I invited the chief pilot of Fairchild to join me for a ride around the patch. The chief was sharp and knowledgeable, and he demonstrated the C-119's landing and takeoff performance capabilities with great expertise. After the last takeoff with the Fairchild chief pilot at the controls, I waited until he called for the gear up. I raised the gear and then *cut off the fuel to number one engine. At this point the gentleman became very upset with my action and vented his feelings on me while he struggled with this engine-out performance that had so endeared itself to my crews.*

After letting him sweat and listening to his blustering, I returned the engine back online and eased the power up. We returned to the base and landed. I reminded him he was flying an empty airplane with only minimum fuel aboard for the engines. How would he have handled forty drums of fuel oil? That was the problem my crews had been struggling with. We returned to the coffee shop and the man from Fairchild and I discussed the problem at hand, and also of a personal note.

As he prepared for his departure, the man from the Fairchild Company left me with this remark: "There is nothing wrong with this airplane that the Douglas Aircraft Company couldn't fix."

Captain Isaacs' logs show his flight time for the military to be 7,350 hours. His civilian flight time was 27,350 hours for a total time of 34,700 hours in the air. He is still a member of the Confederate Air Force with the rank of Colonel. Captain Isaacs loved to fly. He is a perfect specimen of health, but had to turn in his key to the cockpit per the FAA mandatory retirement age of sixty. In his retirement years he spends the summers at his home in Summit Park, located in the Wasatch Mountains east of Salt Lake City, and winters at his home in Arizona.

24

The Ol' Switcheroo

While visiting with one of our newly-hired copilots who introduced himself as Dave Rampton, he told me how he acquired his multi-engine time flying copilot on a C-46 known as the Commando. They flew cargo between the large Hill Field Air Force Base in Ogden, Utah and the west coast. He said he enjoyed flying with all the different captains, and they let him do a large part of the flying. Now and then one of them would pull a throttle back to simulate a single engine and let him go through the single engine procedures. This experience helped him learn the procedures and gave him a feel for how the airplane handled on one engine.

Captain Dave Rampton: *On this particular flight, I drew the captain that all the copilots had warned me about. He was about five feet, seven inches tall, and would hit the scales at 270 pounds. His belly hung over the front of the seat, and he always had to bring his own seat belt extender to buckle up. They warned me if the day ever came that we had a stiff wind down the runway while landing, I was going to buy the farm. "The trouble," they said, "begins when he starts the flare to level off above the runway, because he has to suck in his gut to make room for the control yoke to come back. To accomplish this he has to hold his breath until he has the aircraft on the runway.*

"Now if you are unfortunate enough to have a strong headwind, by the time he gets it flared out he is going to run out of breath and let 'er go. His belly is going to push that yoke forward, and the aircraft is going to nose over. It's just as well you buy the farm. How would you explain an accident of this nature on the report?"

Flying a load of cargo out of Hill we were westbound direct to McClellan Air Base in California, with the directional gyro showing our heading as

270 degrees. The captain was riding shotgun while I did the flying. We had just flown over Reno, Nevada and were coming up on the Sierras. I asked the captain to relieve me at the controls, while I went back to the relief station and did the same. He said, "Take your time son, and while you're back there, check the cargo restrainers."

After I had completed my business, I returned to the cockpit and strapped myself in. The captain advised, "You got her son." Looking out the windshield at the Nevada landscape moving below was always a prime-time event for me. Slowly it dawned on me that something out of the ordinary was happening. What is that city we're approaching? There isn't supposed to be a city there. The Sierras are supposed to be where that city is. Who moved the Sierras? I glanced down at the directional gyro which read 270 degrees, assuring me we were still on a westerly heading. I didn't dare reveal to the captain that I was confused. At the same time I was feeling nauseated, and it's not a pleasing sight when you upchuck all over the cockpit.

Feeling nauseated, I quickly released my belt, and pointed at the controls to indicate to the captain that he was to take over again. He looked abashed as I headed aft, but I didn't have time to explain. Feeling much relieved I returned to my seat. Hardly daring to look out the windshield, I pilfered a peek.

Holy biscuits and gravy, we're over the Sierras. What's amiss here! Where's that city? The directional gyro still read 270 degrees. My stomach was starting to churn again.

The captain looked at me, and then questioned, "Son, are you all right?"

"I'm better than I was, but there is something depraved with the Nevada landscape." Then he started to laugh, and at the same time he got the hiccups. I didn't see anything funny, especially with my captain braying like a jackass. I had to undo my seatbelt and bring him a cup of water before he could get himself under control.

With tears streaming down his cheeks, and his belly heaving like ocean swells, he said, "I gotta tell ya son, you've been had with the old directional gyro switcheroo. While you were in the cabin, I slowly banked the aircraft around to an easterly heading that had us headed back to Reno. Of course the gyro is now reading 90 degrees, so twisting the knob I reset it to read an erroneous 270 degrees, our supposed course to McClellan. With your eyes showing you one thing, and your inclination telling you another, you're not the first one to get a queasy stomach. When you went aft the second time, I gently banked to our original course and reset the gyro to our proper heading of 270 degrees."

The captain's belly oscillated all the way over the Sierras, but this didn't bother me. What worried me was waiting for a wind velocity report from McClellan Air Base.

What's with the Captain

Captain Rampton reminisces about another time when he was flying copilot on DC-3s out of Salt Lake City for Frontier:

There was a captain who enjoyed sliding the side window open enough to cause a suction of air from the cockpit to gush out the open window. Then he would let his necktie stiffly wave out the window, and call for the stewardess. When she stepped into the cockpit, his face would be going through all kinds of contortions while his arms flailed in the air to give the impression the necktie was choking him.

This time, however, when the new stew stepped into the cockpit and saw the captain going through his routine, she asked, "What's with the captain?" Unbeknown to the captain, the clip-on tie he'd worn that day had disappeared high over the Uinta Mountains.

Stud and Hoss

Captain Rampton still laughs about the time he was based in Billings, Montana flying Frontier's Twin Otters over what pilots called the "high line," and others called the "upper U.S." Frontier originally served this route with DC-3s that flew along the Canadian border through such cities as Havre, Glasgow, Wolf Point and Sidney, Montana.

The chief pilot at that time was a tall, lanky dude who couldn't remember the names of his troops, so he called everyone either Stud or Hoss. One night the pilots were out on the town, and one of them suggested they have some fun with the chief. About 1:00 a.m. he called the chief and said, "Hoss! This is Stud. I am sick and will not be able to fly my trip in the morning." Then he abruptly hung up. The chief, not knowing which Stud or which trip the caller was talking about, had to show up for the early morning trip to cover it. It seems everyone showed up for all the flights leaving the chief wondering and waiting for the no-show.

Montana Blizzard

I remember a time, probably in 1963, when Captain Rampton was pulling gear for me. We were on a layover at Billings, Montana in the dead of winter. The wind was gusting hard and the snow had continued throughout the day. Our trip was to depart that evening at six o'clock for Salt Lake City. At that time it would have been dark for over two hours. Knowing there would be problems at the airport, Rampton and I left early and made our way there in the deep snow. With all hands turning to, we cleared the three-foot drifts from around and beneath the DC-3 so we could taxi. With the snow piling up and the wind getting its second breath, the airport authority had shut down all operations for inbound and outbound passenger flights.

The company needed aircraft 135 for an early departure out of Salt Lake City the following morning. With no passengers, dispatch had cleared our flight to operate as a ferry flight, which, translated, means that with restricted runway visibility you can take off with whatever guts you have the courage to muster, subject to the captain's discretion. After engine start we sat in the swirling snow waiting for the temps to climb into the green. The white sheet of wind-blown snow blended into the layered snow and was again starting to drift around the DC-3. The fur-coated agent gave the all-clear and I saluted in acknowledgment. Rampton picked up the mike and called for taxi clearance. The tower answered with "taxi at will, and cleared for take off at your discretion, there is no traffic tonight."

Having flown into Billings many times under similar conditions, I felt quite comfortable with the circumstances. We were able to locate the faint glow of the taxiway lights through the deep snow. As we taxied west, we followed the slight depression of the taxiway. The taxiway lights began to fade in the deep, drifting snow until they disappeared from sight. We continued to follow the slight depression of the taxiway. Rampton strained to locate the north–south runway that crossed our path and would lead us north to intercept runway number nine. Unfamiliar, snow-covered objects just ahead—that turned out to be the airport boundary—indicated we had come to the end of the taxi strip. But which end? When did we cross the north–south runway? Reversing course we followed our own tracks that were fast disappearing in the drifting snow. If we continued on, we would end up back at the terminal…if we could still find it.

We knew the north–south runway had to be somewhere ahead of us. In the black of the night we sat there contemplating our next move. With no lights in sight, and the snow swirling over the aircraft, we felt like we were in the middle of the tundra with civilization a thousand miles away. The tower called to ask if we were off the ground. Rampton replied we were still working our way towards runway nine. Their only reply was, "Good luck."

I pivoted the DC-3 slightly left, and the landing lights revealed the protruding tops of windrows from plowed snow, marking the confines of the north-south runway. As we slowly taxied to the north, the wind-driven snow snaking directly across our path gave the impression we were sliding sideways at forty miles per hour. Then Rampton yelled, "Tallyho!" At last we could make out the dimly illuminated east-west runway lights. Buried under the snow, they resembled Japanese lanterns.

As I eased off the upwind throttle and brake and called for the tailwheel to be unlocked, the strong surface wind pushed the tail of the DC-3 around until we were lined into the wind for an east take off. Everything checked normal on the run up, the tailwheel was locked and the take off checklist was completed. I informed Rampton I could barely make out only two runway lights ahead on each side of the runway (runway lights are spaced 200 feet apart). He concurred. He informed the tower we were on the roll. Straining at the bit, the Grand Ol' Lady gathered speed between the racing Japanese lanterns and lifted off in fine style into the snowy skies of Montana for another uneventful flight to Salt Lake City.

Dave went on to climb the seniority ladder, and as a captain he flew millions of miles. He has joined the ranks of retired airline pilots and makes his home in Syracuse, Utah.

Ringside Memories

How well I remember a trip I flew in the late 1950s on the high line in Montana. The stew mentioned there was a boxer aboard who claimed he fought Joe Louis. After she described him, I knew it had to be Two

Ton Tony Galento, an imbiber who owned his own tavern in the Bronx. Not only did he tend his own bar, he served as his own bouncer as well. A heavyweight contender, he claimed his training consisted of guzzling beer and throwing rowdy patrons out of the bar. I remember him well: short and stocky and built like a beer barrel. Fighters avoided sparring with him because of his noted one-punch knockout. With his head down and in a crouch they could hit him easily enough, but their punches rolled off like spilled soup down a bib and tucker. He was a troublesome fighter to inflict pain upon.

Knowing Two Ton Tony Galento was aboard brought back memories of the golden age of boxing. My dad was a great fight fan who never missed a broadcast of those sporting events. How well I remember sitting by the radio with him as a youth, listening to the exciting introductions by the ring announcer. I'll never forget the enchanting words, "This match is brought to you from Madison Square Garden in New York City." The descriptive blow-by-blow narrative made by the colorful ringside announcer would soon have you feeling you were there in a front row seat. I still think about it.

I *had* to meet Two Ton Tony. As soon as we had blocked in at the terminal in Glasgow, Montana, I hurried into the cabin to meet this renowned boxer and was excited to find he would be continuing on to Havre with us. He seemed pleased that I wanted to visit with him. I related how his bout with Joe Louis seemed like only yesterday. "How well I remember when you rushed from your corner and threw that one punch knockout." "I disa trow it hard enough," Galento responded. "He got up from data canvas and mordered me."

Galento's mind was not on boxing. He was more concerned about the falling snow and ice-covered runways. He asked, "Where youse from?" "Utah," I answered. He broke into a smile, "I'm glad of dat. I wass afraid youse wass one of thoss California pilots who disa know about data snow on runways." As Two Ton Tony Galento walked to the terminal in Havre, he waved to the cockpit. I could see some of his brothers of the Fraternal Order of Elks there to greet him. I would have liked to hear his speech.

Most DC-3 Time

Several articles have been written extolling the accomplishments of Frontier Airline's own William A. McChrystal, who formerly served as senior pilot and flight manager for the Salt Lake City domicile. Captain McChrystal has more documented flying time in the DC-3 than anyone in the world: a total of 17,111 hours, or as Captain McChrystal equated it, an equivalent of sitting in a non-pressurized, non-air-conditioned aircraft continuously for two years. And all this while tooling along at an airspeed of mach .28, which adds up to a total of 2,566,650 miles, or five and one-half round trips to the moon, all in the Grand Ol' Lady.

In 1971, Captain McChrystal was presented the Douglas Aircraft trophy by FAA Administrator John Shaffer, and *Business and Commercial Aviation Magazine writer* Torch Lewis, due to the efforts of Captain Jack Schade and Captain Billy Walker who heard that Lewis was searching for the pilot with the most flying time in the DC-3.

Captain William A. McChrystal (left) sitting in the DC3 cockpit with Captain Al Mooney.

McChrystal graduated as valedictorian from the University of Portland in 1936, and received a scholarship to the Stanford University Law School. Then following his heart, he began his flying career in 1938 at Thompson Flying Service in Salt Lake City where he bought time. McChrystal would chuckle, in his highly dignified manner, when he spoke of the man responsible for his enthusiasm to fly. It was none other than his old football buddy, retired Pan American Captain Charley Blair (actress Maureen O'Hara's husband).

In 1939, McChrystal was accepted for the Civilian Pilot Training program sponsored by the government. He later qualified for additional training through the United Airlines Pilot Training program.

On December 6, 1941, the day before the Japanese attack on Pearl Harbor, he made his first airline flight as a copilot. It was a United charter from San Francisco to Denver carrying Russian Ambassador Maxim Litvinoll and his party. McChrystal laughed when he later recalled that the commissary on that flight included caviar and vodka. He remembered that he was so excited to be flying his first airline flight that the important passengers played a secondary role.

During the war McChrystal was assigned to the Air Transport Command, both in Alaska and in the Asiatic–Pacific Theater, and was employed by Western Air Lines. After the war, the Salt Lake City native resigned his copilot position with Western to accept employment as captain with Challenger Airlines, one of Frontier's predecessors.

Each January, while watching the bowl games on television, McChrystal totaled up his flying time in terms of hours, miles flown, and landings. The total for his entire aviation career equals nearly three consecutive years in the cockpit: 4,674,915 miles (ten roundtrips-plus to the moon) and 20,460 landings. This is a remarkable record considering he spent almost two-thirds of his flying time over rugged, high-mountain terrain in a DC-3. It includes, of course, his own share of hair-raising experiences.

Although much of the glamour of being an airplane pilot deteriorated over the years, McChrystal thoroughly enjoyed his job. "I felt safer flying a jet than driving a car," he said. But he never forgot his old friend the Grand Ol' Lady. "She was first built in 1935," he said, "the first real modern airplane with elbow room and spacious leg room." In remembering his affair with her, he said, "She was part of my life for many years. You can't live with a gal that long without having fond memories." Besides the DC-3, he continued on with Frontier to become type rated in the Convair 240, 340, and 440 series aircraft, the Allison Prop Jet Convair 580, and the Boeing 737.

The many first officers who flew with Captain McChrystal in their early careers felt it a privilege to pull gear for this friendly, unassuming veteran pilot. He was never the strict disciplinarian you encounter when you're unlucky enough to fly with a senior captain who thinks he is destined for greater spheres than the planet Earth has to offer. The cockpit had an air of relaxation, and in this atmosphere you flew a safer trip without the tension that sometimes flows across the pedestal from an exalted captain. He made you feel like a professional, and expected you to do your job. He had first officers standing in line to fly with him. It took a lot of whiskers to hold his line of time; there just were not enough Captain McChrystals to go around.

Vacated Cockpit

In the early sixties, Captain McChrystal and I were assigned to fly a Convair 340 from Denver to Salt Lake City. This would be a quick turn-around. We would deadhead to Denver on the 340, and then pilot it back to Salt Lake City. The flight was loaded and ready for departure when Captain McChrystal and I embarked wearing our uniforms. We stepped into the cockpit to stow our flight kits with the intention of returning to the cabin to ride the cushions in comfort to Denver. The crew flying the trip turned out to be our close colleagues, so we decided to occupy the two observer seats in the cockpit until after take off and slip back to the cabin later.

After the Convair was leveled off at cruising altitude, McChrystal and I returned to the passenger cabin and occupied two seats across the aisle from an elderly lady. Bill was seated next to the aisle and he couldn't help noticing that she looked nervous and watched us attentively. He thought she might need help or have a question, so he leaned over and asked if there was something we could do for her. With a worried expression she said, "I know there is some kind of gadget up there that helps fly these things, but will you two be returning up front to help it land this thing?"

I appreciate the thoughtfulness of McChrystal's daughter Sandy McChrystal Petersen, and Captain Jack Schade, a close friend of Captain McChrystal, in furnishing the above information. The following poem was composed by a Catholic sister many years ago especially for Captain McChrystal, who carried it on his person throughout his career.

A Pilot's Prayer

Valiant Saint Michael be my guide,
As through the clouds I swiftly fly.
My silver wing keep firm and strong,
Make sure my engines droning song.

You who hurled Satan far below,
Aid me to vanquish each winged foe.
Keep through the lit paths of night,
Smooth as an angel wing my flight.

Perils of air, of sea, of land.
Help me, Saint Michael, to withstand.
Grant me a safe swift flight,
Then a happy landing home.

The inscription on the Douglas Trophy awarded to Captain McChrystal reads, "In recognition of an intrepid aviator who, having achieved masterful control of the Gooney Bird, world's most beloved aircraft, is hereby acclaimed as the pilot with the highest total number of hours at its controls above the surface of the planet earth."

Captain W.A. McChrystal passed away July 8, 1992 at the age of seventy-seven.

25

Captain Jack Schade

It seems that in every workplace there is one individual who stands out among his fellow employees, that exceptional someone admired and looked up to. Such is the standing of Captain Jack Schade among his fellow pilots. He was a favorite of all the crews. Captain Schade was known as Frontier's premier storyteller and always had a good yarn to spin. You may have perceived by now from some of the prior plots and tales that Captain Schade made things interesting in the cockpit. I especially remember several trips in the 1950s when we were still flying DC-3s across the mountain empire.

Captain Schade, a man with a tremendous appetite for gooseberry pie, was always off the airplane at Riverton, Wyoming before the props had stopped windmilling. I would try to keep up with him as he hot-footed it for the little airport cafe, but I soon stopped as some of the passengers thought I was chasing him. Captain Schade never ordered a regular meal, it was always gooseberry pie.

When anticipating the captain's arrival, the cook kicked in the afterburners on the oven to make sure the gooseberry pie would be waiting to appease the captain's appetite. When they saw that it was Schade easing the DC-3 to a stop on the ramp, they quickly cut a big wedge and set it on the counter before backing away. Nobody dared interrupt him until the dish was clean. He always requested a second slice, and back then pie was cut into four grand slices.

It is rumored that some copilots always checked by calling ahead, fearing dire circumstances if the little cafe didn't have gooseberry on the menu that day.

I remember the time we arrived at Riverton late, and our turnaround time was shortened to the extent we didn't have time to enjoy Jack's favorite pie. Jack asked me to hurry into the cafe and pick up a couple of wedges and we would enjoy pie after getting off the ground. Feeling quite prosperous as I had just received my salary, I asked the waitress to cut a whole pie four ways and slip it into a container.

The captain let me fly the first leg and after we leveled off at cruise altitude I asked if he would please pass me a slice.

"Where is it?" he asked. I answered that I had slipped it behind his seat.

"I thought all that was for me. Where's your pie?"

"In the container behind your seat, I think."

He handed me the empty container, and trying to look repentant said, "I made a mistake." He hadn't fooled me. When Captain Jack smells homemade gooseberry pie, he's like a Piranha going after dessert: he had finished off the entire pie. Of course, I got to fly an extra leg.

Multiple Uses for the Oxygen Tube

Oxygen requirements for the DC-3 consisted of a flexible rubber tube with a fitting that you inserted into the oxygen outlet located on the side panel next to each crewmember station. On the other end was a pipe stem that you held in your mouth when oxygen was needed. Besides having a great appetite, Captain Schade carried a great thirst around with him. When the oxygen tube wasn't being employed, he had discovered other uses for it.

There are two fuel selector valves, one on each side of the pedestal located between the pilots which was a convenient place to set beverage cups. When flying after dark, the captain kept the cockpit lights turned to a low setting. He would then sneak his oxygen tube across the pedestal and let it slide into the copilot's cup. With the long rubber tube taking the place of a straw, he would soon empty the contents. The victim was never quite sure why his cup was always empty. He would request another drink from the stew and the whole process repeated itself. A few stews thought some of the copilots had hollow legs; and it was rumored that other copilots swore off drinking any beverage in a DC-3 cockpit.

Captain Schade denies he ever thought up any uses for the oxygen tube other than to supply oxygen to the crew. He will stand all day with hands in his pockets and hold a straight face while bantering with you about his innocence.

A rumor circulated that the oxygen tube could be used as a water pistol. A search for the source of this rumor led to Captain Schade. When asked to demonstrate this new feature of the oxygen tube he slowly acknowledged, "I'll tell you how it works, but just because I know how it works doesn't mean I used it for such." He then proceeded to explain. "You unplug the hose from the outlet and drop it into a container of water. You then suck on the pipe stem and the water is drawn into the nose. After selecting a target, you pinch the hose at the pipe stem, plug the other end into the oxygen outlet, aim the pipe stem, and release the pressure. The built-up pressure in the hose from the oxygen will propel the water like a squirt gun."

"What do you usually aim at?" he was asked.

"Usually at the stew's posterior as she leaves the cockpit—but that doesn't mean I would do such a thing."

Author's note: The practice of propelling water from the oxygen hose took place in the days of the Grand Ol' Lady. Today, you would be publicly humiliated, fined, and sent to jail.

The Copper Halo

There was always relentless weather to fly through in the DC-3 days. We couldn't go high enough to fly above it, so we would tighten our belts and punch through the areas appearing to have the least minimal weather. One time when I was with Captain Schade, an electrical storm was strutting its defiance by shooting lightning bolts all over the sky.

Captain Schade called the stew to the cockpit and asked if she was wearing her grounding antenna.

"I don't know what you're talking about," she replied.

"Hold up there a moment, and I'll make a grounding antenna from copper wire for you to wear on your uniform hat. We don't want our stew getting knocked on her fanny by Mother Nature. Hand me your hat." Captain Schade formed a halo with copper wire, then ran a strand of wire down from the halo, and fastened it to her hat. As the stew left the cockpit, her halo shown brightly above her hat. To inquisitive passengers she happily replied, "I'm to wear this anytime we are near an electrical storm." Soon the word was out that one of Mother Nature's little angels was safely guarding the airways with grace and charm.

It Happened

Captain Schade said that airline pilots can sometimes be a little fiendish with their sense of humor. He related the following anecdote:

> *Braniff had just finished redoing the interiors of their aircraft and were painting the exteriors with a variety of different colors. While waiting in line for departure at Denver Stapleton Airport, a Braniff jet taxied out and fell in line. It was painted with multiple colors flowing in a wave-like pattern from nose to tail. Suddenly on our radios we heard, "Hey Braniff, who puked all over your airplane?"*

Burp Cups

Captain Schade was a true professional. But when the two of us shared the same DC-3 cockpit, open season was declared on anything that broke the monotony of a long trip.

Flying into Albuquerque on one of those extra warm days when the upper air was super-heated, we suffered the wrath of Mother Nature as she spread a path of continual turbulence over our route. After landing, our usual custom was to grab a quick meal and pick up a box lunch for the stew, who had to remain aboard the aircraft. We hurried to the hospitality of the excellent restaurant in the old terminal to enjoy our fill of delightful Mexican cuisine at its best.

As we polished off our chili rellenos, Captain Schade ordered a container of split pea soup to go. I knew it was going to be open season on our next leg. Arriving at the aircraft, Captain Schade handed the box lunch to the stew, keeping her occupied while I smuggled the split pea soup to the cockpit.

Departing Albuquerque, we climbed to 12,000 feet and leveled off. Even at this altitude Mother Nature was still in an ill-tempered mood. I wondered if she knew about our open season. Captain Schade hit the stew call button, and I knew our plan was about to unfold.

After the stew made her presence known in the cockpit, Captain Schade explained that the combination of Mexican food and turbulent air had left his copilot with a queasy stomach. Would she please fetch a burp-cup?

When she looked over at me I was prepared. Captain Schade had coached me until I was blue in the face, which was red now because I had been holding my breath. As I leaned over in my seat holding my stomach, she rushed to the commissary and returned with a burp-cup. Captain Schade suggested, "It would help if you brought him a couple of wet towels." As soon as she left to get the towels, we poured the green split pea soup into the burp-cup. To make it more realistic, I wiped some of it around my mouth and chin, letting it drip back into the full container.

Rushing back into the cockpit, she tried to hand me the towels. Feigning more nausea, I ignored them. When she reached for my full burp-cup, I clutched it and quickly drank some of the contents. She screamed and in a shrill voice demanded, "What are you doing?!" Not looking too well herself, she then ran from the cockpit.

Dreaming up beguiling pranks of this nature made short legs out of long legs, and fortunately, when the stews realized they had been had, they laughed about it and warned all the others to be on the lookout.

Christmas Eve High Above Albuquerque, New Mexico

This delightful Christmas story was taken from the original copy as written by Captain Jack Schade:

> *Unmarried pilots or those without children would volunteer to fly holiday trips for their fellow pilots who had children, so they could spend the Christmas holiday with their families. This event took place on Christmas Eve 1951.*

> *I was married without children and my copilot was in the same situation, so we signed in to fly the Salt Lake City to Albuquerque run on Christmas Eve. I arranged for my wife to go along so we could be together on Christmas Day.*

My copilot was a big, rugged, good-looking cowboy from Wyoming. He was a real man's man. Our trip departed from Salt Lake about 6:00 p.m., making several stops en route before arriving at Albuquerque.

A Spanish custom in the southwest is to light candles that are set in a sand base at the bottom of a paper sack similar to those used for carrying groceries. These are known as Luminarios. On an earlier trip to Albuquerque, I had noticed how impressive these displays looked on the public and university buildings.

As our flight approached Albuquerque, the night couldn't have been more beautiful. There was a full moon, twinkling stars and the air was smooth as silk. I looked at Jack Kettler and asked what he thought about a sightseeing trip over and around the city to give our six or seven passengers a look at the Christmas decorations. He was in agreement and then suggested that he would be happy to get a fruitcake out of his bag to share with passengers and crew. This sounded like a good idea. Then he suggested a cup of coffee to go with the cake. Another good idea. Then the clincher. He had brought along a bottle of bourbon for a little toddy on Christmas Day. We thought that under the circumstances, everyone should be offered coffee royal with their cake and tour of the city.

As we began our flight over the city, it was decided that if the food and drink service was good enough for the passengers, it was good enough for the crew. I believe the statute of limitations will prevent the Feds from getting me, and if that isn't protection enough, they made me retire 17 years ago on the age 60 requirement. Nevertheless, this is a memory I'll keep forever, when flying a DC-3 was just about the best thing a man could experience.

Very British

Captain Jack Schade tells a story that involved pilots for Western Airlines (now Delta Airlines). In the mid-1940s shortly after WWII, a Western DC-3 departed Salt Lake City en route to Pocatello, Idaho. A winter storm warning was in effect. Captain Schade relates the history of this flight:

An extensive weather system had blanketed the area with a very active snowstorm, but indications were that it was beginning to move out of the area as ceilings and visibility were slowly improving. Solid instrument conditions existed, but minimums for takeoff and landing were being reported, so this particular flight was dispatched to fly north originating out of Salt Lake City.

The captain was a man who had flown in the British Royal Air Force during WWI, and came to the U.S. after the war. He became a United States citizen and was hired as a pilot by Western Airlines. The copilot was a native of Salt Lake City and quite an outstanding athlete at the University of Utah. The aircraft was the reliable DC-3.

The flight departed Salt Lake City in the evening and headed north toward Ogden, Utah. Western's dispatcher called the flight to advise that the weather at Ogden was zero-zero, Salt Lake City was now below minimums for return, but Pocatello was above minimums and suggested that the flight proceed to Pocatello.

On arrival over Pocatello, the flight was informed by radio that the weather was down to zero, zero for ceiling and visibility, ceiling being the height of the cloud base above the ground. The flight requested the weather at Idaho Falls north of Pocatello. The station radioed back that every station from Salt Lake to Great Falls, Montana was under blizzard conditions. The picture was beginning to look a little bleak because a big factor now was the amount of fuel on board.

The captain, who was typically British in his use of language—always courteous, very proper and businesslike—said to the copilot, "Mr. Bowers, I believe our best option is to hold here on the west leg of the radio range and wait for improvement." They flew west for a few minutes, executed a procedure turn, and reversing course, flew back to what is known as the "cone of silence" over the center of the radio antenna. They reversed course and repeated the flight pattern again. In the meantime, they kept requesting current weather reports. Each time the response was, "No change. We can't see anything beyond a few feet." While the captain was doing the flying, the copilot was watching the fuel gauges creep toward the big E.

As the copilot later related this story to me, he said the knot in his stomach kept getting bigger and tighter, and he had to work to keep his concentration on where they were and what they were doing. He had just about accepted the idea that they were going to have to do the very best they could with a controlled crash landing in the vicinity of the airport as the fuel was insufficient to go anywhere else. These thoughts were interrupted when the station called to say a slight improvement seemed to be occurring with the *weather. The captain said he appreciated this information and to please keep him advised if and when they noticed a change—either way!!*

About five minutes later, the report indicated the weather seemed to be letting up somewhat and the copilot, who was still eye-balling the fuel gauges so intently that his eyes were watering (the needles were in the middle of the big E), exploded with "Oh, hell! Oh, pardon me sir, how about we make the approach with what's being reported?"

The captain's reply, "Mr. Bowers, I like the trend and I think we will be in good shape here in a few minutes, so relax and things are going to be just fine." Sure enough, in about five minutes the weather report was "ceiling about 400 feet, visibility approaching two miles." The captain flew a perfect range approach, despite static caused by the precipitation, as he listened to the on-course signal through his headphones. They broke out of the weather, lined up with the snow-covered runway, touched down light as a feather between the soft glow of runway lights reflecting from beneath the snow, taxied into the terminal area, and shut down the engines.

After a few minutes of trying to get his shaking legs and voice under control, the copilot said, "Captain Monty, I don't know when I've been so damned scared in my life!" He told me the captain gave him a strange look and said, "You know, Mr. Bowers, I was beginning to be a little concerned myself."

Very British, don't you think?

Captain Schade retired from Frontier over seventeen years ago and yet his memory still brings up the good things that linger in the past.

He talks very little about his combat experiences flying the long 3,000-mile overwater run to Japan and back to Guam. When he does talk about flying combat missions, it's always about the friends who didn't make it back.

He never failed to return to his island base on Guam, but it was often under shaky circumstances. Like not always bringing all the parts of the Superfortress back with him, leaving them scattered over The Land of the Rising Sun as a reminder of his warm reception by the Japanese military.

The last mission over hostile territory for Captain Jack Schade was the "Show of Force Flight." On September 2, 1945, four-hundred-thirty-five B-29s circled over the land of the rising sun while the Japanese formally signed surrender terms aboard the USS *Missouri*.

General James H. Doolittle wrote the following about the B-29s: "The Navy had the transport to make the invasion of Japan possible, the ground forces had the power to make it possible, and the B-29 made it unnecessary."[10]

B-29 Superfortress.

Motivation to be an Aviator

Captain Jack Schade: *Lindbergh's flight across the Atlantic in 1927 created an instant hero for my grandfather. He was a member of the Salt Lake Police Department and worked out of the county jail which was located east of the present City and County Building in downtown Salt Lake City.*

We lived in a rental unit north of the jail which made it very convenient for my granddad to visit with us. My dad always had a supply of home-brewed beer stashed away and a crock of the same maturing in our basement. I might add that my granddad was an Irishman, so he never hesitated to accept when my dad offered him a "cold one."

During these visits, my interest was with granddad's revolver. He would empty the cylinder of its ammunition and let me just sit and hold the weapon. His conversation always got around to aviation and his hero, Lindbergh. I began to pay attention to him and listen intently to what he was saying. When he saw my interest, he began to include me in the adult conversations. Soon, he started to bring balsa rubberband-powered model airplane kits to me along with aviation pulp magazines such as *G-8 and his Battle Aces*. Now that he and I had established a common interest, he would let me ride with him in his Model T Ford police car as he made rounds. Somehow we always ended up at the old Salt Lake Airport where we would visit with mechanics or pilots, or, if there was no one to talk with, just walk around and gaze at the airplanes. A kind of camaraderie developed between us, and I now had two heroes. My desire to be a pilot was born through this wonderful relationship with my grandfather and lived on long after he was gone.

Some years later, in 1939, I became a very disgruntled eighteen-year-old. I wasn't making much money, and most of it went into the family "pot"—too much discipline at home, I thought, so I decided to move on. I talked with a Navy recruiter about becoming a flying cadet, and being told I would need to complete at least two years of college, I went to check out the Army Air Corps. I was told, "Sign here, and we'll see that you get to fly." I signed, my parents signed, reluctantly, I might add, but my mind was made up. On 1 September 1939, I sailed out of San Francisco Bay for the Panama Canal, assigned to the 74th Bombardment Squadron at Albrook Field.

I became an apprentice airplane mechanic. Our aircraft were B-18s, a Douglas twin-engine aircraft based on the DC-2 design. We also had A-17 attack types assigned to the squadron. I finally passed the examinations that classified me as a 1st-AM, a mechanics rating that meant I was still a private in rank, but my pay went from twenty-one dollars a month to about eighty dollars a month.

The only way to qualify to be an aviation cadet was to get some college years behind me. I planned to fulfill my two-year enlistment, return to the States and attend the university, but WWII wiped out all my plans. All enlisted personal were frozen into their present units and positions. When Pearl Harbor was attacked, it was assumed the Canal would also become a target.

My squadron flew patrols in B-18s from a jungle airstrip near the border between Panama and Costa Rica searching for the enemy thought to be approaching the Panama Canal. About March 1942, we transferred to Guatemala City to continue patrol flying and added antisubmarine searching over the Caribbean area. The squadron was now supplied with

Liberators and the early model B-17s. In addition, our flights were extended to the Galapagos Islands off the coast of Ecuador. This meant an overnight stay, then back to Guatemala the next day.

Since the unit was still at peace-time strength, we all learned to do jobs other than our primary assignments. So in addition to being a crew chief, I became an aerial gunner, radar operator, aerial photographer, and parachute rigger. About this time I was promoted to staff sergeant. My pay remained the same, but this rank became a bonus when I finally got into the aviation cadet program as a NCO (non commissioned officer) and classified as an aviation student. The drill instructors, whom I sometimes out-ranked, gave me extra privileges.

I was classified for pilot training at Santa Ana, California. After I had completed ground school training I was transferred to Visalia, California to begin flight training in the Ryan PT-22. My basic flight training took place at Chico, California in the Vultee BT-13. I completed my advanced flight training at Pecos, Texas in the UC-78. At Pecos I was commissioned, but more importantly I pinned on the wings of a military pilot.

My next stop was Hobbs, New Mexico, for B-17 training. I felt good about this assignment as I was acquainted with the airplane from my time spent with it in Central America, but this was not to be. The B-29 was now operational and became my new assignment. My orders were to report to Walker Army Air Corp Base at Hays, Kansas to become part of a crew to train for combat crew operational readiness. I met ten men (boys actually) and we were going to become a team. We became operational about February 1945 and shipped out as a group to the southwest Pacific theater. Guam, one of the Mariana Islands, was to be our new base.

As a crew we flew twenty-five missions attacking targets on the Japanese homeland. We thanked God when the Marines secured Iwo Jima as this gave the flight crews the possibility of landing on a runway instead of ditching in the ocean. While securing Iwo Jima, the Marines suffered a very high casualty rate that would save the lives of thousands of air crewmen. We used the facilities twice, both times due to a three-engine operation without enough fuel to make it home. A round trip from Guam to Japan was about 3,000 miles, approximately fourteen to fifteen hours flying time.★

When a B-29 landed on Iwo Jima, an engineering/maintenance officer would ride a "follow-me jeep" to check the airplane over at the end of the

---

★**Author note:** Over two thousand battle-weary B29s limped into this haven at sea.

landing roll to look for excess damage. He would give either a "thumbs up" which meant taxi to a hard stand, or a "thumbs down" which meant that a tractor standing by would be hooked to the nosewheel and the airplane would be towed to the junk yard on the beach where it suffered the indignity of being stripped for its spare parts.

On one daylight mission, about seven feet of our horizontal stabilizer and elevator were shot off by anti-aircraft fire. After we had determined the airplane was controllable, our next concern was whether or not we could bypass Iwo Jima. This airplane was a part of our team and we weren't about to take any unnecessary risk of it ending up in the junk heap on Iwo Jima.

We scrutinized the remaining fuel on board and checked the distance and cruise control charts. We thought maybe we could reach the small island of Tinian or Saipan, or maybe even Guam, the most distant island, if the tailwind remained steady. Everything held together, and we had hearts full of gratitude when we saw Guam coming over the horizon. With the fuel gauges indicating zero, we acknowledged the welcome screech of the tires on the runway with silent prayers.

Our airplane was once again made airworthy by parts salvaged from other B-29s, and we all managed to remain together until the war ended. We had the privilege of flying it in the Show of Force with Marine and Navy aircraft to impress the Japanese of this country's air power as the surrender documents were being signed to end the war.

I was returned to the States in November and left the service after six years. Many years later, while on the ramp at Hill Field Air Force Base in Ogden, Utah, I happened to spot my unforgotten friend sitting forlornly among the many parked aircraft. As my heart swelled, tears welled in my eyes at the flood of memories that rushed through my mind of good and bad times endured together. How she got there, I don't know; what happened to her, I don't know. She was like a phantom in the dark; like a dream she was there and then she was gone. I like to think she came to me for one last visit. She'll never be forgotten.

Author note: A giant in her time, the B-29 with her four 2,200-hp Wright 18 cylinder radials, each with two exhaust-driven turbochargers gave her a maximum speed of 357 mph, and a service ceiling of 36,000 feet. Carrying a bomb load of 12,000 lbs, she could range up to 3,250 miles. When Major General Curtis LeMay made the decision to bomb Tokyo by night with incendiaries from altitudes between 4,900 and 9,200 feet, the results were devastating. Millions of inhabitants evacuated the cities, finding refuge in the hills as some 267,000 structures burned to the ground. Fourteen B-29s went down, many of them ditching in the ocean.

When the war ended, 3,960 B-29s had rolled off the assembly lines. The Superfortress with her wide wing, and long clean body was the most imposing of all WWII bombers.

After working at a couple of different jobs I didn't particularly care for, I managed to get hired by Western Airlines. I still didn't have enough college credits to my name, and since this was a requirement, I had to use the old ploy of "not what you know, but who you know" in order to bypass this prerequisite. After nearly a year with Western, they began furloughing and I was out of a job. In July of 1947 I landed the best job a person could hope to have when I was hired by Challenger Airlines (later becoming Frontier Airlines). I spent thirty-four memorable years with the best airline and the best employees there ever were.

Looking back, I'm convinced some greater power looked at this lad and said, "This guy is going to need a lot of help, so he'll be my project." Somehow, doors were opened and decisions were made for me that have made this time in aviation the best years of my life. I wouldn't have it any other way.

Hired by Challenger Airlines in 1947, Captain Schade was among the dedicated pilots who were there in the beginning and who experienced the pioneering of hauling mail throughout the Rocky Mountains. There were those who said Challenger would disappear with the coming of the mountain blizzards, but Captain Schade was among those who were greeted by the first spring thaw with the promise of better flying conditions.

Schade accrued 13,462 hours in the DC-3, most of it in the mountain west. He retired in 1981 after serving Challenger/Frontier for thirty-four years with a total flying time well over 30,000 hours. But still caught in the DC-3s enchanted spell, he came out of retirement to once again captain the Grand Ol' Lady on designated mail runs and charter flights through the Rockies. And never refused the opportunity to crawl into the left seat of a DC-3 bound for Alaska with a rush order of helicopter parts for Rocky Mountain Helicopter. Whatever and wherever he flew, copilots vied for his line of time.

Captain Schade, now in his seventies, stays busy tending to the needs of his home at the base of the impressive Mt. Olympus in Salt Lake City. He serves as a colonel in the Confederate Air Force and finds time to arrange luncheons for retired pilots who appreciate the opportunity to reminisce about the golden years of flying.

Wedding Bells High Above Denver

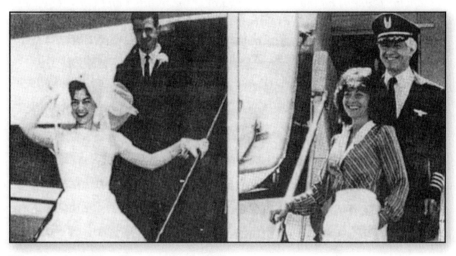

Wedding in 1959... The couple in 1981

Flying at 3,000 feet above Denver, Colorado, Captain Dick Hoffman and First Officer Marion Tongish eased the throttles back until the manifold pressure read 20 inches on the gauges. After slowing the DC-3 to its minimum speed they began a gradual descent over the city. May 15, 1959 turned into a superb morning for this memorable occasion: The airborne wedding of Frontier Captain Pete Lamkin and his beautiful bride, Frontier Stewardess Janet Curry. Captain Chick Stevens recounts the wedding:

> *Captain Lamkin first saw his future bride at the Alamosa, Colorado air terminal while waiting for an exchange of passengers and cargo. Upon asking the agent who the good looking gal in the lobby was, he was informed that she was a new stew based in Denver. Pete thought Jan was the prettiest girl he had ever seen and he didn't want to waste any time. Stepping out from behind the ticket counter to make her acquaintance he tripped over the weigh-scales and sprawled face down on the terminal floor.*

As he nonchalantly regained his feet and dusted himself off, he could hear the last boarding call for his flight and rushed to the airplane to assume his cockpit duties.

Back in Denver, Pete checked the stewardess schedule and bid the same schedule the beautiful stew would be flying for the month of July. After flying together as crewmembers for six days, Pete knew she was for him and asked Jan to marry him. She accepted.

Since it was the DC-3 that had brought them together, Jan thought it would be nice if the Grand Ol' Lady would lend her presence to the wedding party. Captain Lamkin had reservations regarding the weather and other unforeseen problems; he was especially concerned with the publicity such a wedding might generate. They hoped to make this a reverent occasion with only family members and a few close friends. A Methodist minister refused the invitation to perform the wedding ceremony because of all the unknowns, but the chaplain from Lowry Airfield was happy to oblige.

On the morning of the wedding, the weather refused to cooperate and spread scud and low ceilings over the Colorado landscape. Rumors had been leaked to the Denver Post, who contacted Frontier, but Frontier feigned complete innocence. The wedding was moved up one hour to avoid any unexpected guests.

The front row of seats in the cabin were removed, and, with the wedding party all aboard, Captain Hoffman (whom Pete had enjoyed flying with) and Tongish (Pete's roommate) requested clearance to climb on top of the cloud layer. As the wedding party climbed into the blue sky, they noted that the clouds below were fast breaking up, and the air had become as calm as a soft summer morning. Captain Hoffman reduced the power and when the cabin sounds of the Grand Ol' Lady became less noisy, the chaplain called for reverence, and the ceremony in the sky commenced high above Denver.

After serving as a charter pilot and instructor for Monarch Aviation in Grand Junction, Colorado, Captain Lamkin hired on with Frontier in 1956 at the age of twenty-two. He checked out as captain on the DC-3 at age twenty-five. Pete served Frontier as a check airman and later became manager of flight training for propeller-driven aircraft. After serving Frontier for many years in the training department, Pete followed his heart and went back to flying the line.

Captain Lamkin and Janet are now retired. Janet has become a successful artist and shows her work in various galleries throughout the west.

27

Flight 32 is Down

We had just landed at our small hub in Riverton, Wyoming, and I could see the flight had arrived from Billings, Montana. The flight from Denver was in the pattern. Ed Radford, my copilot, and I hurried into the crewroom to enjoy a short visit with the crew from Montana, who turned out to be Captain Ken Huber and his copilot Daniel Gough. Captain Huber and I had recently attended a six-month check in Denver and had become quite well acquainted. He was a straightforward individual who attended to business and yet had a friendly disposition that made one feel comfortable to be around him. Although it had not been my privilege to fly with him, word coming out of Denver was that Huber was an excellent DC-3 pilot with many hours of experience flying the rugged Rockies.

In the early hours of March 13, 1964, my phone was ringing off the hook. I groped for it and managed to get the receiver to my ear. It was my friend Captain Dick Ure. I woke up when I heard the words, "Flight 32 is down at Miles City, Montana, and Ken Huber was the captain." The word *was* presented an ominous foreboding. I knew it was bad and going to get worse. Flight 32 impacted the ground less than two miles from the Miles City Airport during an instrument approach in adverse weather conditions. Crews who had experienced flying that far north had their own ideas regarding the sudden termination of flight 32: *Low level icing.*

The CAB (Civil Aeronautics Board) made a thorough investigation into the cause of the accident, and File No. 1-0004 reveals the result of their report. The crew arrived at the company's operations at Billings between 6:30 and 6:45 p.m. to prepare for the flight. At 7:25 p.m. the captain received a weather briefing from the U.S. Weather Bureau. A cold front was approaching Miles City and gusty northwest winds would persist with turbulence and moderate icing. Squalls would prevail in the area. The forecast for Miles City called for ceilings 2,000 feet above the ground, with visibility 3 miles, light snow, wind northwest 20 knots with gusts, occasional visibility 1 mile, light snow.

Flight 32 departed Billings at 8:01 p.m. It had been cleared to fly the airway to Miles City VOR (navigational radio fix) at an altitude of 7,000 feet and estimated arrival over the Miles City VOR at 8:42 p.m.—approximately 41 minutes en route. Nineteen minutes after departure, Great Falls Air Route Traffic Control Center relayed the latest weather at Miles City to flight 32: Ceiling 1,000 feet above the ground, visibility 4 miles, light snow showers, wind northwest 25 with gusts to 35, and cleared the flight to make an instrument approach into the Miles City Airport.

At 8:45 p.m. the flight advised Miles City Flight Service they had passed over the radio fix at 8:45 and were starting the approach. They also contacted the company radio at Miles City and advised they had crossed over the VOR and gave their fuel load aboard as 485 gallons. The company radio advised there was no reported traffic in the area and the wind was 20 with gusts to 30 knots out of the northwest. The flight advised they would be on the ground in 3 minutes and they would need a rudder lock (locks the large rudder in place when on the ground in gusty winds). The station acknowledged. This was the final transmission between the flight and the company station agent.

Flight 32 reported to Miles City Flight Service that they had passed over the VOR inbound to the field and planned to land northwest into the wind. This was the last radio contact between the flight and Flight Service. In none of the transmissions from the flight was there any mention of operational distress or of weather conditions encountered.

At 8:50 p.m., aircraft number 442 struck the ground in a slight nose-up attitude. The investigation showed the aircraft to be in a landing configuration. After initial impact the aircraft began to disintegrate and continued moving for a distance of about 600 feet. Fire developed and a major portion of the aircraft was destroyed.

Fire and other damage made it impossible to determine the readings of many of the instruments. However, the captain's altimeter was at the proper setting. The location of the crash site showed it to be on its proper course to the field. Examination of the maintenance records of the aircraft indicated that maintenance had been current. No item that could logically be related to this accident was discovered. Fire at impact and the time interval before people reached the crash site made it impossible to determine if airframe icing had been present at impact. A record special observation was taken at 8:55 p.m., five minutes after the accident, which said in part: indefinite ceiling 500 feet, sky obscured, visibility 1 mile, light snow showers, temperature 32 degrees, wind northwest 20 gusting to 30 knots.

One witness, a technician who was inspecting the ground navigation radio facility, reported he saw an aircraft that he could identify as a DC-3 pass overhead toward the airport at a height of approximately 1,000 feet and about 600 feet north of his position. According to the witness, the aircraft appeared and sounded normal at this point. He estimated that wind gusts were 35–40 knots, "or maybe more," that the wind was strong enough to move small rocks on the ground and the driving snow was very wet. Another witness, who was in a parked car about 3 ½ miles south of the airport, did not see or hear an airplane but did see a red flash in the sky, and the entire sky to the west was lit up. He noted a gusty wind from the north with snow or sleet. A pilot witness was in his home in Miles City about one mile southeast of the airport. He heard an unusually loud noise from an airplane which lasted four to eight seconds and ended abruptly. He described the weather as moderate wet freezing snow with wind gusts of 30–40 knots.

The investigation revealed no improper procedures and/or malfunctions of any of the related equipment pertaining to this accident. It must be kept in mind that strong winds with blowing wet snow and low ceilings could and probably did significantly distort both sounds and sightings as described by witnesses. The evidence indicates that the aircraft flew over the VOR at approximately 8:48 p.m. about 1,000 feet above the surface. The aircraft at this position, according to the witness, appeared and sounded normal in all respects. Yet, the point of impact was located only 1.7 miles from the VOR where the minimum descent altitude should have been approximately 400 feet above the ground.

Because there is no evidence of any failure or malfunction of the aircraft or navigational aids, the board cannot state with any degree of certainty the reason for the unexplained departure from the minimum descent altitude.

It was determined that weather conditions in the vicinity of Miles City were conducive to moderate to heavy airframe icing in clouds and precipitation. Strong gusty winds over the rough terrain would likely have produced moderate to severe turbulence in the area. Under these conditions, large ice accretions on the wing surfaces would have become a serious detriment to airspeed and altitude control, especially after the landing gear and flaps were extended. With such an accumulation of ice, it is possible that prior to or at the time the flight reached its minimum descent altitude (400 feet) above the ground, the descent could not be arrested without a serious loss of airspeed. A situation of this type, it is recognized, could necessitate lowering the nose of the aircraft to regain airspeed, resulting in a rapid loss of altitude and operation below a safe terrain clearance altitude.

In conclusion, the CAB determined that although existing weather conditions were conducive to airframe icing, there is insufficient evidence available to support a definitive finding in this area. Similarly, the evidence will not support any conclusion that the pilot committed a gross departure from proper piloting techniques by attempting to conduct the final portion of the approach through visual reference to the ground. The board, therefore, is unable to determine the reason for the aircraft's departure below the approved minimum descent altitude.

Captain Kenneth C. Huber, age 42, had a total piloting time of 15,335 hours, 12,830 in DC-3 aircraft. He was properly certified, rated, and checked. He was unusually well experienced, currently, in landing scheduled Frontier Airline's DC-3s at the Miles City Airport.

First Officer Daniel H. Gough, age 25, had a total piloting time of 3,539 hours of which 1,355 hours had been as first officer in DC-3s. He was properly certified, rated, and checked. Captain Huber and First Officer Gough had flown together, as a crew, on numerous Frontier flights into the Miles City Airport.

Stewardess Dorothy Ruth Reif, age 22, had been employed by Frontier Airlines since October 13, 1963. Passengers aboard the flight consisted of one company employee and one paying fare passenger.

The argument held by many Frontier pilots was that the aircraft had descended into an area of low-level, severe icing that can make an aircraft uncontrollable in a very short time. Captain Dick Ure reported similar conditions at the same location several months later. The ice accumulated so suddenly he was unable to climb out of it. With ice obscuring the windshield, he had to open the side window for any ground reference. Unable to check the descent, he commented, "I was gratified the runway was beneath me when the aircraft ceased flying. Ice had to be chipped from around the main entrance door before they could open it."

In later years, the contention of some crews was the possibility of a microburst. A microburst is an intense column of downward rushing air that extends to the surface and then mushes out in all directions. When the aircraft descends to the runway in a landing configuration, and while flying at lower airspeeds should it enter this rush of air, it could possibly experience a large increase in airspeed. Then, at a critical point, the headwind may suddenly become a tailwind that destroys the lift on the wings. This sudden shift in the wind causes the aircraft to make an involuntary descent—possibly with cataclysmic results.

To the inexperienced pilot, the mountain empire presented an adverse geographical area that Frontier pilots flew daily. Pilots flying in the high, rarefied air continually had to contend with mountain waves, rotor clouds, and extreme downdrafts on the lee side of mountain ranges. This was the only fatality in the forty years of Frontier's existence involving a paying passenger in scheduled service.

28

Early Day Jackson Hole Approach

In my early flying career, Jackson Hole, Wyoming was a favorite layover for me. If possible, I always bid to fly the Jackson Hole trips. In the early years the airport did not have a navigational facility. Later a VOR (Visual Omni Range) was installed which sometimes prevented us from making an approach in marginal weather because of its high landing minimums—and when we did, it consumed a great deal of time. If approaching Jackson Hole from the south and they reported low ceilings in the Jackson area with the base of the Tetons still visible, we looked for familiar landmarks through breaks in the clouds that we could safely descend through. By doing this we hoped to avoid being trapped in the weather over Jackson and find it necessary to shoot a time-consuming VOR approach.

A favorite approach, with weather permitting, would be to let-down into Star Valley, Wyoming, a beautiful, large valley about thirty-five miles south of the Jackson Hole Airport. From there we followed Highway 89 north until we reached the southeastern shore of the Palisades Reservoir. With clouds capping the gorge we followed the Snake River through what is called the Grand Canyon of the Snake, a twisting, deep gorge that could sometimes be a little exciting. After that it was just a matter of finding enough room to skim below the clouds, and follow the river until seeing the airport. The passengers loved it; many of them were motion picture celebrities commuting to their vacation retreats.

Approaching from the north, we could sometimes make out the imposing Grand Teton Peak rising above a sea of clouds in a stately manner. This verified the previous weather reports of overcast ceilings in the Jackson area. It would be necessary for us to take advantage of any large breaks in the weather if we intended to descend below the clouds in visual conditions and find our way to Jackson. It was sometimes necessary to take advantage of breaks as far north as Yellowstone Lake in order to descend beneath the clouds, if the opportunity presented itself. From there, we followed Highway 89 into the northern approaches of Jackson Hole until reaching Jackson Lake. We then followed the Snake River until over Moose (a small settlement), at which point we lowered the landing gear, completed the landing checklist while holding 180 degrees on the compass, until we could spot the Jackson airport.

Even though we couldn't see it due to the restricted visibility, we knew Blacktail Butte would be to our left and craggy Grand Teton Peak, rising to 13,770 feet would be but a short distance to our right. Where else in the United States could you find more breathtaking scenery, all for the regular price of an airline ticket?

In later years, they installed an instrument landing system at the airport, and spoiled all our fun. Making approaches into Jackson Hole these days is duck soup. I remember flying to Jackson with a copilot who was on temporary assignment to Salt Lake City to cover additional flying time. He had done most of his flying out of the Dallas, Texas area and other parts of the south. He was unfamiliar with the mountain empire, but eagerly looked forward to seeing the Tetons. But this day Jackson Hole was like an immense tub filled with bubbly suds, as moisture-swollen clouds filled the entire valley.

As our instruments told us we were over Jackson, the company radio told us we had landing minimums. We shot the instrument approach in gray swirling clouds that obscured the mountains to their lower basis. When breaking out beneath the weather, the rain-streaked runway was on our nose. The inviting scent of wet sage filled the cockpit—a special greeting from Jackson Hole. The copilot was disappointed because he had hoped for a better scene. I said, "Maybe next time."

When the next time was here and you couldn't have asked for a more perfect evening. The receding sun sent bursts of light rays through the saddles and canyons of the Teton peaks spreading shafts of light over the Jackson Hole Valley.

Grand Teton Peak had a dusting of snow that refracted the light rays into a glowing splendor that encircled the peak with a crown of gold, as if to declare "The King is in residence for the evening." While descending through 13,000 feet, the copilot murmured, "I don't like it."

"Don't like what?" I asked

"I don't like descending below the elevation of these mountains."

"If we don't descend below these mountains, how are we going to land at the Jackson airport?"

"I preferred the other day, when everything was obscured in clouds, and I couldn't see the mountains."

"I thought you wanted to see the mountains."

"I don't like looking up at them, I'd just as soon be looking down at them. This big hole is surrounded with high mountains."

Then it dawned on me that flying the flat lands, he had never experienced mountain flying. This first-time experience was a little overwhelming. If he had been doing the flying, we would have had to shoot him down.

I advised, "You just relax, and read me the checklist. This old Mountain Master we're flying will get us in and out of there like an old maid going to her wedding." After his inaugural flight, he was ready for more.

Flying into Jackson in the wintertime was especially inspiring. The valley would be covered with deep snow and it was a true wonderland. I have seen the terminal wrapped in plastic to protect it from snow that would sometimes drift as high as the rafters.

Walking from the plane to the terminal in a man-made snow trench, with snow rising above your head, gave the illusion you were walking through a jetway. It's not uncommon for the temperatures to drop to −40°F. I don't know what the record is, but it's well below that. Jackson Lake freezes over solid. I remember watching a large crawler Caterpillar making its way across the frozen lake.

It was difficult to locate the airport with everything covered in deep blankets of white snow; it was almost like flying in a total whiteout. After New Years, the Jackson Hole Airport personnel gathered

Christmas trees and outlined the runway with them. This would help us see the runway from further out, and it also helped us judge our height above the runway while landing. Thinking about it now, I still miss flying into Jackson.

Convair 580 at Jackson Hole Airport, Wyoming

Springtime in the Rockies

Flying the Allison Prop Jet 580 over the Rockies in the springtime could sometimes be a little challenging. Mother Nature likes to mix all the ingredients together—summer, winter, and spring—then dish it at you all in one setting. Uncomfortable squirrelly winds and the most severe icing levels await you. As temperatures rise, you encounter constant turbulence from massive buildups of cumulo nimbus clouds that hover over your route waiting to pelt you with machine-gun-like hailstones.

Fighting the elements on an April midnight was like patching a dinghy full of buckshot: There was no end, but it had to be done. With lightning streaking from cloud to cloud and cloud to ground, and areas of scattered hail over our route, the radar was finely tuned to guide our way this stormy night. The airwaves were full of radio calls to air traffic control, asking for vectors around weather and discussing the best route of flight. In the midst of it all, an anxious female voice was heard asking for assistance to avoid the worst of the weather.

Capitulating to courtesy, the airways became silent until a male voice chided her for flying on a night such as this. Another then commented, "You ought to be home cooking in the kitchen." Without hesitation she answered. "I wish I was."

Regardless, her professional manner and radio phraseology sent a message that she was a pilot of considerable experience. She had no problem holding her own with the best of the sky pack that night.

Solitary Snooze

After everyone had deplaned the Night Hawk flight, the doors were buttoned up on the Allison Convair 580 for the night. The mechanics began their inspection of the aircraft, preparing it for its Early Bird flight. About 2:00 a.m., an ashen-faced mechanic stood before his supervisor, Tink Thiese, and stammered, "I'm not going near that thing. It's making weird noises and when I crawled up into the rear cargo compartment, I could hear heavy breathing in the cabin."

Thiese dropped the forward airstairs, entered the cabin and began to check the interior of the aircraft with his flashlight. The mechanic was casting a wary eye while huddled close to Thiese who now shown his light to the rear of the cabin.

The light zeroed in on a huge individual sprawled over two seats producing wheezes and snorts comparable to a steam locomotive working an uphill grade.

Still snorting and grunting, he was gently led off the aircraft and sent on his sleepy way. He never realized he had been the sole occupant of a secured aircraft. The stewardess, amiss in her final check of the cabin, kept her fingers crossed to ward off a complaint that never materialized.

Strangers In The Dark

I believe my most unpleasant experience involving an individual I'd never met before took place in Billings, Montana. As soon as our passengers had deplaned from the Convair 580, we rushed to check out. The hour was late, and the motel restaurant where we overnighted would soon be closing.

We checked in at the motel and barely made it to the restaurant on time. After ordering, we set our bags behind the counter and went into the restroom to wash up. My copilot, Al Harris, had finished drying his hands and as he stepped out the door, flipped the light switch off.

With hands that were soaking wet, I felt my way in the dark towards the light switch. At that moment, the door partially opened and I could make out the features of my copilot, but then he stepped back. I was ready when he made his second appearance. Grabbing a handful of water I waited. When he stepped in I flipped the water in his face, and with soapy hands, grabbed him around the neck in a slight choke hold and held on.

Another man entered the restroom and switched the light on, so I looked over to see who it was. Only it wasn't a stranger, it was my copilot, Al. Horrified, I looked at the person I still had in a choke-hold. Cowering before me was a small gentleman about seventy years old and wearing a gray flannel suit. His eyes looked like saucers. I attempted to wipe the water off his suit, but only made it worse. Stumbling over my words I made an apology. The little guy yelled, "I'm alright! I'm alright!" Then he turned and rushed out of the restroom.

My copilot had retreated to the lobby and along with the stewardess they were telling all. With everyone in the lobby now aware of my blunder it sounded like a brawl out there. Mortified, I opened the door and humbly stepped out to face my audience.

While seated at our table, Al proceeded to give his version of what had happened. He said as he opened the door the second time, the little fellow ducked under his arm and sauntered in. He knew what had happened when the little guy cried out in terror.

It didn't soothe my feelings any when he added, "Then the little guy with big eyes rushed out with beads of water running down his suit and disappeared out the first exit he could find. He's probably home right now telling his wife that some nut wearing a uniform is in the Holiday Inn restroom choking the patrons as they unsuspectingly make their entry."

For some reason I passed on dinner that night, and being the poor sport that I am, I didn't invite the copilot to make any landings the following day.

Several trips later, we were on a layover in Denver. That evening Al came to my room to watch a movie on TV. Al had removed his shoes and left them at the foot of his bed. When the opportunity arose, I slipped his shoes into my overnight bag. After the movie I watched Al return to his room in his stocking feet. He didn't ask about his shoes and I didn't volunteer anything.

The next morning Al knocked at my door and asked if I had noticed his shoes laying around. I got down on my hands and knees, looked under both beds and around the room and then innocently told him I couldn't find them.

He said, "I must have set them in the hall when I unlocked my door, and apparently someone has walked off with them."

I volunteered, "With the black socks you have on no one is going to notice. If they do, they'll just think you are another airline pilot who got dressed for an early morning trip."

With time growing short, we caught our transportation to the airport and checked in at the crewroom for our trip. One of the dispatchers asked Al where his shoes were. Al said, "Somebody walked off with them."

With a big grin on his face the dispatcher said, "You guys flying these early morning trips ought to give yourselves more time to wake up in the morning. Captain Dave Rampton showed up here one morning wearing house slippers. Some of you wear socks that don't match, and one captain was wearing suit trousers with his uniform coat and hat, and now you show up with no shoes at all."

Al didn't think this was very funny, and with everyone asking where his shoes were, he was starting to feel a little self-conscious. I waited until he walked over to pick up the latest weather, and while he was occupied, I slipped his shoes into his overnight bag. When it was time for us to walk down the flight line to our waiting aircraft, I asked, "Are you sure you don't have your shoes? Passengers who will be boarding our trip will see you down there walking around the aircraft without shoes. They're going to wonder what kind of copilots this company employs. Are you sure you didn't pack them with all your other clothing? Maybe you ought to check your overnight bag again; while you do that, I'll climb aboard and check the cabin."

When Al boarded the aircraft, he was wearing his shoes. I knew I was going to be safe as they were starting to board passengers, and I had gotten even. (Kinda.)

Sharing Goodwill

The flight out of Salt Lake City to San Francisco with stops at Elko and Reno, Nevada turned into an entertaining curiosity. Our call sign was United/Frontier, meaning that the route belonged to United but Frontier had contracted to fly it. After parking the Prop Jet 580 at Elko, preparations were made for the passengers waiting behind the fence to come aboard. It was always fascinating to watch a certain brunette and her companion. Their departing embraces and affectionate kisses looked like they were meant to last a long time. She was always the last one aboard the aircraft.

Upon our arrival at Reno, she was the first to deplane and as she hurried into the arms of her waiting companion, it was obvious he wasn't her brother. When we returned that afternoon from San Francisco to Reno, we observed this same couple in passionate embrace expressing their good-byes. She was the last one aboard.

After our return to Elko she raced off the aircraft into the arms of her first companion. Who were these waiting companions? We'll never know, but the merry-go-round continued for several weeks.

Standoff at the Elko Restroom

During the Prop Jet 580's descent in preparation for landing at Elko the crew observed dust from a strong westerly surface wind. Elko lies in a valley filled with hilly terrain surrounded by mountains. With the wind following the contours of the terrain, the 580 waltzed with the turbulence like a frivolous fat lady tripping the light fantastic.

After the passengers had deplaned, First Officer Gary Winn informed the captain he had to make a latrine check. The captain said, "I'll join you." After they entered the terminal and made their way into the restroom, the captain (who wishes to remain anonymous) made his move. He quietly waited until all the restroom patrons had left, then, checking to see the shoes of First Officer Winn firmly planted on the floor beneath the latrine partition, called, "I'll see you on board." Opening the door to exit the restroom he said, "Oops! Sorry about that," pretending he had bumped into someone.

Then he slammed the door and stomped back into the restroom. In a gruff voice he mumbled, "Them damn airplane pilots. I've got a humpback mule that rides better 'n' that thing they're flyin'. If I couldn't make that critter ride better 'n' that, I'd get a job herdin' sheep."

The captain then watched the feet of First Officer Winn slowly elevate until they disappeared behind the latrine door. Again in a gruff voice, he muttered, "The more I think about it, the madder I get." After kicking a metal waste container he stomped out slamming the door behind him.

Returning to the cockpit, the captain watched and waited for the return of his first officer. As departure time drew near, he was beginning to be concerned. He watched as two station agents pulled a covered baggage cart out of the freight room and parked it next to the boarding stairs of the aircraft. The first officer quickly slipped out of the cart and gingerly made his way up the airstairs and into the cockpit without looking back.

Nothing was mentioned of the incident until they were at cruise altitude over the Ruby Mountains. With time to relax, First Officer Winn commented, "That cowboy you bumped into as you left the restroom doesn't like the way we fly. It's a good thing you left when you did, because he was ready to shoot somebody."

"How come he didn't shoot you?"

"He didn't see me because I was standing on the commode."

"Do you always stand on commodes?"

"Only when I hear a mad cowboy."

Later the captain told him what really happened, and First Officer Winn, being the good sport he is, laughed. (Copilots have to do that.) After 25 years, Winn still hasn't forgotten this incident.

Wind Power

At an outlying station a Prop Jet 580 had an inoperative GTC (Gas Turbine Compressor) and with a battery attempting to go west, they found they were unable to spool up the number two turbine. Using a little ingenuity, they waited for the arrival of the next 580. They explained their problem and the crew agreed to help them spool up the turbine.

They aligned the arriving 580 directly in front of the disabled 580 and, changing the blade angle on the huge props, they slowly backed to within thirty feet of the disabled 580. With both crews in radio communication, the crew in the lead 580 slowly moved their thrust lever (throttle) forward on their number two engine. The resulting prop blast began to slowly turn the large four-bladed prop on the disabled aircraft. With the lead aircraft now spooled up to a high power setting, and the violent prop blast directed at the number two turbine of the disabled aircraft, whose propeller was now rotating at a high rpm from wind power, they got a light off and the engine spooled to its normal revolutions.

They flew the aircraft to Denver where maintenance could correct the problem. The prop blast from the lead aircraft took the place of the faulty auxiliary power unit and provided the forced air to rotate the prop which in turn rotated the turbine.

Solving problems in the field saved the company a great amount of money and downtime on airplanes. The company was not always aware of the money the crews saved them through such schemes, and it was never discussed in crewrooms for fear of repercussions from the Federal Aviation Administration.

Gremlins

One time while flying a Boeing 737, I had initiated the letdown from flight level 330 (33,000 feet) in preparation to land at St. Louis. Descending through flight level 230 (23,000 feet), I heard an unfamiliar sharp report from within the aircraft, and then sensed we were beginning to depressurize. I increased the Boeing's rate of descent hoping to descend through 14,000 feet before the decreasing cabin pressure climbed to the preset setting that automatically deployed oxygen masks in the cabin.

Hundreds of masks hanging down from the overhead panel make the cabin look like a rubber jungle and the mechanic, whose job it is to repack them in the overhead receptacle, madder than a biting sow. As I thought about this, I increased the thrust levers hoping to increase the supply of pressurized air from the packs to the cabin. But to no avail; the masks deployed on schedule.

After we descended through 10,000 feet it was necessary to decrease the aircraft rate of descent to 500 feet per minute so our passengers' ears could adjust to the altitude changes (just like in a DC-3). Because of the lower rate of descent it was necessary for approach control to give us special handling with radar vectors to merge us into the flow of heavy traffic waiting to land—an extra workload for the controllers.

Parking at the concourse, I saw the friendly FAA agents waiting to greet me. I knew they were from the FAA, because they were rubbing their hands together and smiling. They asked me about the problem with the pressurization. I answered, "I lost it about thirty miles out and if I knew why, I would be happy to tell you."

I knew the company would be scrambling to get another airplane ready because this one would not be making the scheduled turn-around flight back to Denver. The flight attendants would be upset if they had to stand up their dates in Denver.

I recorded the maintenance report in the aircraft logbook and gave an oral report to the lead mechanic. My crew had already departed for parts unknown. Knowing the entire world was upset with me (life as an airline pilot has its occasional downside) I caught the limo to our layover abode. On the way, I relaxed in the back seat of the airport limousine and reminisced about the good old days. At least with the DC-3 we didn't have pressurization problems. We just chewed Doublemint chewing gum to help our ears adjust.

After a full day of troubleshooting without locating the "gremlin" that caused the pressurization problem, the company assigned the copilot and me to ferry the aircraft to our major maintenance base in Denver. It was another two days before Denver could correct the problem. As it turned out, they ran a pressurization check on the aircraft while it sat on the ground. This is similar to inflating a balloon—air is pumped into the interior to pressurize it. After the cabin pressure had climbed to a higher ratio of pounds per inch, an access door on the underneath section of the fuselage leading to the radio compartment slightly buckled, and let the pressured air inside escape through the breach as though it were a dump valve. When the pressure dropped to a lower value, the access door popped back to its normal contour. This was a tough one to solve, but our exceptional maintenance department did it. The problem was remedied on all Boeing 737 aircraft.

Afterburners

After our arrival at Grand Forks, North Dakota, we all felt weary from a long day of flying the Boeing. My crew, First Officer Fuzz Parten and three flight attendants were eager to get some much-needed rest. Our place of abode lay just over the border in East Grand Forks, Minnesota. After check-in at the American Inn, Fuzz and I went to find our rooms. The American Inn is a beautiful structure in a country setting. Being fairly large it was with some difficulty that we located our rooms. As we opened the doors, one of the flight attendants called out from down the hall that the key would not unlock her door. Fuzz and I thought it was odd that she was billeted on our floor as they usually checked the flight attendants into another part of the Inn.

She insisted this was her assigned room. (For security purposes, the keys are imprinted with a different code than the room number.) It would be a long walk back to the front desk so Fuzz, a registered locksmith, said he'd open the door for her, and softly added, "I hope I don't get in trouble for doing this." Fuzz unlocked the door and opened it. Sitting up in the bed glaring at us was the meanest-looking individual that Fuzz or I had ever seen. Then he bellowed just like he looked. Fuzz mumbled, "Sorry, wrong room." With our feet in afterburner we back pedaled out of there and Fuzz slammed the door.

We determined that now would be a good time for us to be in our own rooms, and we told the stew that she was on her own and had better get her room straightened out at the front desk. She called on the phone later, apologized for the misunderstanding, and explained she had been on the wrong floor in the wrong wing.

An announcement made by one of our male cabin attendants was overheard on the PA system by Captain Jack Schade as he taxied the Boeing to its assigned gate. "Ladies and gentlemen, for your safety, please remain in your seats with your safety belts buckled until we arrive at the jetway and the seat belt sign is turned off."

After a pause he said, "Ladies and gentlemen, I can hear the rattle of buckles as you are attempting to undo your safety belts. I must remind you the seat belt sign is still on. For your information, I'm at the rear of the aircraft, and I have the only key to the forward exit of the aircraft from which you hope to deplane."

29

Tragedy

One copilot in particular who made things interesting in the cockpit looked like a fighter jock and was an excellent pilot. He had purchased a rare WWII fighter, the P-38, known as the Lightning. It had made its presence felt in every major theater of the war and was especially renowned for its air supremacy over the Japanese Zero in the South Pacific.

A conversation I had with one of our older captains who had flown P-38s during WWII revealed that on rotation from the runway, if an engine failed at that critical moment, the sudden torque from the high power setting on the remaining engine had a tendency to roll the Lightning over on to its back.

If you were faster than greased lightning at this critical stage, you might be able to prevent the roll by retarding the power on the good engine, then slowly increasing the power enough to keep the Lightning above terra firma until returning to the runway. A precarious maneuver at best.

On one particular trip that my friend and I crewed into Dallas, Texas, we discussed this critical failing of the P-38. He explained that he was well aware of the inherent gremlin, and if the day ever came that he had this problem, he hoped to be a survivor.

Just one month later that day came. He flew the Lightning into Salt Lake City for maintenance. After completion of the work, he lined up on runway 32 and started the takeoff roll. At liftoff, the right engine abruptly failed without warning. The Lightning was seen by witnesses to roll over on its back and augur in. He didn't have a chance. The subsequent investigation revealed that asbestos shielding had torn loose and plugged the air intake of the carburetor causing an immediate stoppage of the engine.

I've included this account simply because it keeps coming to my mind. Trying to remember the facts renews melancholy memories of other friends who have made their way through the blue horizon early, but that's the way it is; and for some of us life continues on.

A Hundred Million Reasons

B-737 taking off

Flying the Boeing 737 at flight level 330 (33,000 feet), I search below to locate the Sweetwater River in the South Pass area of Wyoming, and also to recognize the North Platte River as it lazily meanders out of southeast Wyoming into Nebraska. After the South Platte branches into the North Platte, it is known as the Platte. It continues its nomadic course through the former prairie lands of Nebraska, and discharges into the Missouri River. I remember that its hard rimrock banks once served as a roadbed for the westward movement. On the north bank of the Platte, long stretches of the old covered wagon trail left by Mormon pioneers still endure from when they slowly made their way to the land of Deseret. I wonder if a certain pioneer ever imagined that in the future—from an altitude of 33,000 feet—one of his great-grandsons would follow in just a few hours the same trail that it took him several months to complete.

Thousands of Oregon immigrants made their way along the south bank of the Platte River. As I study the Sweetwater in the South Pass area of Wyoming, the trail is still visible due to the deep ruts made by covered wagons over one hundred and fifty years ago.

Flying with the jet stream on my tail, I approach a ground speed of ten miles per minute. In two minutes I will have traveled twenty miles. Twenty miles traveled in a wagon train would be one of their better days. As I gaze at the landscape below, I can enjoy an orange from California, a hot steak from Nebraska, a baked potato from Idaho, and pudding made from Central American bananas. I can have a drink of cold fresh milk served directly from refrigeration compartments. And I can adjust my cockpit-seat for more comfort. Surely with over a dozen settings I can find a position to suit my pleasure while I enjoy a panoramic view of hundreds of miles of the finest scenery on earth.

If radar tells me there is a storm ahead, I may deviate a hundred miles or so to give the paying passengers a smooth ride. It will cost only a few short moments.

As I scrutinize the trail below and ponder the hardships my great-grandfather endured, I wonder about the passenger who grumbles because the busy flight attendants cannot keep his coffee cup filled. I wonder about the passenger who doesn't like his steak medium or who complains because we will be a few minutes late at our arrival destination, and this because we circumnavigated foul weather. I say, "Let them eat dried beans and crusty biscuits with lumpy gravy day after day, and wash it down with warm, tainted river water while trudging footsore along a trail that seems to have no end."

Sometimes I wonder why I'm so fortunate, and I am. I have a hundred million reasons to be thankful, and I am.

Sometimes I'd Rather Not Wake Up

On frequent layovers at various cities, I, like many pilots, would lay the phone book on the nightstand at night so the following morning I could confirm which city I was in—and which hotel room. All with good reason.

At one layover I got up during the night to pay a visit to the blue room. Unable to locate the light switch, I proceeded in the dark. On the way I knocked over a lamp, shattering it. Opening the door and stepping in, I found myself being mugged. I put up a good fight and got an arm lock on my assailant.

Through all the commotion I heard yelling and pounding, and then realized it was the occupant in the next room asking me not to walk on the walls. Sheepishly, I realized I was in the closet with my uniform coat draped over my arm still in an arm lock.

It was frustrating trying to orientate myself in a room that wasn't the one I thought I was in. I thought finding a light switch would end my confusion. Stumbling into an end table, I was able to grab the lamp before it fell, but knocked the shade off in the process. I grasped the lamp tightly with feelings of relief. As my vertigo horizon stabilized, I felt for the switch and clicked it on. Dissecting the room with a weary eye, I saw that I was in an Atlanta, Georgia hotel instead of the Phoenix, Arizona layover hotel I thought I was in.

Ever since then, I memorize the location of light switches. Wherever I think I am, I am able to turn the lights on—unless I forget what I "memorized." I offered to reimburse the motel management for the damage I caused while "defending" myself. The manager laughed and said "This is not unusual for airline pilots." I wonder what they meant by that...

Unfortunately, this is not an isolated incident. In defense of my fellow pilots who have experienced similar episodes, you have to realize that with exhausting jet lag, the many different motels and hotels we stay at with rooms sometimes located next to noisy elevators or below those occupied by 350-pound sumo wrestlers who walk in their sleep and snore in Japanese, makes a man want to grab his walking papers and run.

"I Lost Control"

An acquaintance who managed a motel at one of our overnighters in Billings, Montana loved to cruise the countryside. He racked up more fender benders than the Indianapolis Speedway. After telling me of his latest experience in a new Thunderbird, I refused to ride with him anymore.

He explained how he drifted onto the shoulder of the road and, with his quick reflex action, overcorrected when trying to get back onto the highway. He found himself shooting across both traffic lanes into a gas station, knocking over two pumps and causing a spontaneous discharge of sparks that ignited a fire. Then the Thunderbird slid sideways back onto the highway and collided with the rear duals of a semi-trailer, knocking them off. He dryly commented, "After hitting the semi I lost control."

How true his description of the wreck is cause for speculation, but I did see the wrecked Thunderbird. It resembled a vehicle that had been in a demolition derby. I thought it might be prudent for him to continue preparing his excellent prime rib dinners and leave the driving to others.

Is a Hard Landing a Botched Landing?

A hard landing is not necessarily a bad landing. Much depends on the factors involved at the time of the landing, such as limited runway visibility, high crosswinds, especially if it's gusty, and short runways with reported poor braking action. Sometimes you may have all these factors combined to test your piloting skills. Rather than over fly a lot of precious runway looking for that smooth touch down, it's just best to plant her on. So in rare cases, a hard landing is a good landing. But to the passenger, a hard landing is a hard landing.

From those who do not understand proper landing techniques, such as flight attendants, you must suffer the wrath of the uninformed. Stews will shoot daggers at you while you're trying to slip off the plane unnoticed. A few passengers may nudge each other and give a wink as you pass by.

Our ground school scuttlebutt informs us there is a way to avoid all these smirks. You trade hats with the copilot so as he deplanes with all the gold braid on his hat, folks will just naturally think he is the captain. In their way of thinking he is the one who makes all the landings. That being the case he is the one who will have to suffer the indignities. But then this has caused even more complications—some copilots refuse to give the hat back without a fist fight.

I haven't had this problem. For some reason my hat is much too large for any of the copilots to wear. I haven't rationalized why, but regardless I've come up with a solution to this dilemma of trading hats. After a hard landing, I make a PA announcement and in my good-humored way I proclaim, "Ladies and gentlemen, I hope you enjoyed the landing. Some days we have good days and some days we have bad days; today was one of my good days."

31

A Challenge Met

Captain Bert Hall began flying in July of 1937 at the old 21st South airport in Salt Lake City when Vern Carter was the manager. He loves to reminisce about the days before WWII. There are still a lot of old pilots who will reminisce with this jump-start to their memories. Some of Captain Hall's early flights began with the Curtiss Wright Jr., a pusher numbered NC11831, with its 45-hp Saekely engine. He made it his ambition to fly everything he could possibly get his hands on, and many of the younger generation may not recognize some of these early aircraft. Most were made of wood and fabric and were built before WWII. They were the pride and joy of the old aviators.

The following list comprises the aircraft flown by Captain Hall, who was kind enough to let me search through his records; I've tried to be accurate with their classification and the type of engine installed:

The J-2 Cub with Continental A 40-hp engine; Cub E-2 with its Continental 40-hp engine; Curtiss Robin with Curtiss WR 185-hp engine; Luscombe 8A with a Continental 65-hp engine; Waco F with Kinner 125-hp engine; Monocoupe with a Lambert 90-hp engine; Pitcairn with Wright 250-hp engine; Fairchild 21 with Kinner 100-hp; Waco VKS-7 with Continental W-670 240-hp engine; Aeronca with Le Blond 85-hp engine; Eaglerock with Curtiss 225-hp engine; Waco YKS-7 with Jacobs 225-hp engine; Cessna Airmaster with Jacobs 165-hp engine; Kinner Sp'st with Kinner 100-hp engine; Culver Cadet with Continental 75-hp engine; Fairchild 22 with Ranger inline 200-hp engine; Rearwin with Franklin 80-hp engine; Porterfield LP with Lycoming 65-hp engine; Fairchild 24W with Warner 145-hp engine; besides the Bonanzas, he has flown various models of the older Beechcrafts with the Jacobs 285-hp engine, including the Pratt & Whitney 450-hp engine; Cessna 195 with 300- hp Jacobs engine.

Captain Hall was commissioned an ensign before Pearl Harbor, and during WWII he served as a commander in the United Stated Navy. An accurate log of the different aircraft he flew during his Navy career is recorded in full, and the number is astonishing.

The Commander persuaded flight chiefs around the country to give him the green flag to check out aircraft based at their airfields. He loved a challenge and made it his goal to check out at least one new aircraft every month. After checking out the capabilities of an aircraft, the commander would sometimes roll it over on its back and practice flying a rectangular course while inverted.

One aircraft in particular that many pilots know existed, but know little about, was the Douglas transport designated the DC-5. The first model rolled off the production line February 15, 1939—a total of twelve were built. Even with its high wing, it could pass as the younger relative to the DC-3 sitting on a tricycle. Many parts were interchangeable. Captain Hall states that the DC-5 was built to fill the needs of the short-range routes. There were three models built: the passenger model could accommodate 16 to 22 seats; the cargo transport was ideal with its low profile not requiring special loading equipment; the executive model with its club interior specially built for William Boeing, president of The Boeing Aircraft Company, as his personal aircraft. You could have your choice of either the Pratt & Whitney Twin Wasp or the Wright Cyclone radial engine. With war clouds hovering near, the DC-5 was discontinued when the assembly line changed over for the production of needed SBD Dauntless dive bombers.

The DC-5s flown by the Navy and Marines were designated the R3D. Commander Hall flew all three models for a total of 122 hours, and 46 minutes.

Following is only a partial list of the more noted aircraft flown by the commander while serving in the Navy: O3U-1 & 3 series with P&W 1340-D 550-hp; SBU-2 P&W 1535-98 with 750-hp; SU-2 P&W 1690-C 600-hp; NS-1 LYC 220-hp; N3N series 1&3 WR 78-8 235-hp; NP1 LYC 680-8 235-hp; OS2U-3 P&W 985-AN-2 450-hp; GH-1 P&W 985-AN-6 450-hp; J2F-5 W 1820-50 950-hp; SNJ series 2, 3, 4, 5 P&W 1340-36 & AN-1 550-hp; JE-1 P&W 1340-38 550-hp; JRF-6B P&W 985-AN-6 450-hp; F4F series 4 & 4B & 7 P&W

1830-36 & 86 & 205 1200-hp; G36-B P&W 1830-86 1200-hp; JRF-5 P&W 985-AN-6 450-hp; F2A-3 W1820-40 1200-hp; TBF-1&1B W 2600-8 1700-hp; GB-1 P&W 985-48 450-hp; BT-1 P&W 1534-44 825-hp; SNC-1 W 975-28 450-hp; J4F-2 RNGR6-440C5 200-hp; OS2N-1 (S) P&W 985-AN-2 450-hp; F4U-1 P&W 2800-8 2000-hp; SB2A-4 W 2600-8A 1700-hp; F6F series-3 & 3B P&W 2800-10 2000-hp; R50-5 W 1820-40 1200-hp; FM-1 P&W 1830-26 1200-hp; TBM-1 W 2600-8 1700-hp; R4D series1&3&6 P&W 1830-92 1200-hp; GB-2 P&W 985AN-1 450-hp; R50 series 3 & 6 P&W 1830-84A1 & W1820-87 1200-hp; JRC-1 Jacobs 755-9 225-hp; SNB-1 P&W 985AN-1 450-hp; PBM-3R W 2600-12 1700-hp; PB2Y-P&W R-1830 1200-hp; R5D series 1, 2, 3, 4, 5, 6, P&W-3, 7, 11 1350-hp.

Some of the aircraft flown were of the same category and same engine, but differed in the modification designation of the engine. All told, Captain Hall's records show he has flown over 107 different aircraft including the previously named F4F Wildcat and F6F Hellcat built by Grumman and the F4U built by Chance Vought. Included in his logs are two identical aircraft built by different companies: the TBM torpedo bomber built by General Motors, and the TBF torpedo bomber built by Grumman. Commander Hall continued on to master the multi-engine transports. This doesn't include the DC-3s or Convair series and the Allison Propjet 580, nor the Boeings he flew while employed with Frontier Airlines. What an amazing number of assorted aircraft flown in one lifetime! Could this be some kind of record?

A comment might be made here that it would be a difficult task to find a more qualified pilot in any major airline to occupy the left seat of the front office. It was a privilege to sit in the front office with Captain Hall who was quick to share the knowledge he had gained from many years of pushing throttles on a variety of aircraft. Crews particularly benefited from his knowledge on how to out wizard Mother Nature.

He wanted those Pratt & Whitneys finely tuned, the props synchronized and no time wasted in flying from point A to point B. If you didn't, it was *shiver me timbers*.

The Five Finger Checklist

Captain Hall passed on some very useful information. "When encountering a problem with your aircraft, use the five finger checklist." Then pointing at the five fingers on his hand he illustrated.

"Number one, fly the airplane."

"Number two, determine what's wrong."

"Number three, fly the airplane."

"Number four, rectify what you can."

"Number five, fly the airplane."

An undetermined number of pilots over the years became so engrossed in solving a problem with their aircraft that they neglected to check their flight status and flew into mountains or descended into swamps. I might add that with emphasis directed at flying the airplane, these type of tragic events are mostly a thing of the past.

The Phantom with Eerie Hands

Commander Hall relates an amusing experience that happened during WWII when he was flying an R5D transport (the military version of the DC-4) with military personnel aboard. It was a black night. He tied a white glove to each side of the control yoke, and with the autopilot manipulating the controls, he hit the cabin attendant call button. Then he and the first officer quickly hid in a forward storage compartment where they awaited the arrival of the attendant.

The female cabin attendant stepped into the cockpit and found the crew missing. The florescent glow from the instrument lighting radiated off the gloves, giving them an eerie glow. She watched as the yoke continually moved about as it responded to the commands from the autopilot. Her impression was that eerie hands were manipulating the yoke. With a whispered gasp she froze, slowly backed out of the cockpit in stark terror, and quickly returned to the cabin.

Feeling a little passive, the commander sent his first officer into the cabin to soothe her feelings and explain what she had seen. The first officer entered the cabin just as she was telling (with great apprehension) the other cabin attendants that a phantom with eerie hands was flying the ship.

The continuation of the trip was a long haul for the flight deck crew: there were no refreshments brought to the cockpit by the cabin attendants.

Not My Fault

Captain Hall tells of one proud pilot who flew for the Lockheed Company in the 1930s who had a spotless record of no incidents while flying the Lockheed 10, and intended to keep it that way. The day came that the Lockheed 10 lived up to her reputation by swapping ends in a perfect ground-loop scraping a wing tip and damaging a couple of ribs on her outer right wing. Not wanting his employer to know of the ground-loop, and trying to cover the fact that the Lockheed had gotten away from him on landing, he talked an off-line mechanic into agreeing to repair the damaged wing. The mechanic insisted on one provision: the captain would supply the two outer wing ribs for the repair.

The captain put in a call to the Lockheed plant and requested the parts. Lockheed was very meticulous and wanted the history leading to the failure of the two ribs. The captain, not identifying himself in hopes of remaining incognito, said, "Never mind the cause of the failure, just send what I've requested." Lockheed insisted that without a detailed history the order would not be filled.

Acquiescing, the captain said, "We got into a kind of tight situation, I took care of my side of the aircraft, but the copilot failed to take care of his side."

Don't Worry Your Mind Me Lad

Captain Hall tells about the time the big four-engine PB2Y Coronado flying boat had been refueled and readied for its lengthy patrol when the fueler realized he had added more fuel than requested by the aircraft commander. He explained the fuel problem to the ship's crew chief. The salty old chief answered, "Don't worry your mind me lad. Besides the regular fuel load, the captain always likes a hundred gallons added for him, I like a hundred gallons added for me, and we like a hundred gallons added just for the hell of it. And you'd be muddled, me lad, how many times we've made it back just for the hell of it."

32

Chief Pilot Scott Keller

The Postage Stamp

Captain McChrystal's notes refer to a newspaper article during WWII telling of a forced landing by an Army Troop Carrier C-47/DC-3 in Immigration Canyon just east of Salt Lake City.

McChrystal explained that there is a good-sized rock pile, called the Wasatch Mountains, along the eastern borders of the city. As the C-47 climbed over the canyon loaded with troops, both engines suddenly lost power and quit, caused by a malfunction in the C-47s antiquated cross-feed system and a broken line. Unable to make a restart, the pilot desperately searched the rock pile for a suitable landing area to set down the beleaguered C-47. The only apparent flat spot was a reservoir. But a water landing didn't appeal to the pilot so he picked out a postage-stamp sized pasture, the only other spot available, and dead sticked his ship successfully into it. The newspaper account said one man suffered a broken leg when he jumped from the aircraft onto the pasture. The others walked away. The plane had to be dismantled and trucked out of the pasture.

The crew's commanding officer flew up from San Antonio to investigate the incident. After taking one look at the C-47 in the pasture and shaking his head, he commented, "Only a dumb second lieutenant could put that airplane in a pasture that small and walk away from it."

After the war, that second lieutenant turned out to be Captain Scott Keller, Frontier's future chief pilot for the Salt Lake City domicile. Captain Keller served many years as flight manager, then was transferred to Denver to serve as a vice president.

Stretched DC-3

Trends for today's aircraft companies are to design, draft, and toil for years to introduce the perfect, large passenger jet. After it all comes together, the prototype is rolled out for the flight test which confirms to all the aeronautical engineers, draftsmen, metallurgical geniuses, electrical engineers, hydraulic engineers, and accountants, on down to the water boy, that they have a winner. With the successful completion of flight tests, borne out by the prototype, the fruits of their labors go into production, and deliveries begin to worldwide markets who covet the right to advertise that their inaugural flight will be the first of a new generation of aircraft.

Then, it's back to the drawing board for all the geniuses, to stretch that bugger even longer, to make the payload still greater and more efficient. Then the question is always asked, "Why didn't they stretch it in the first place? It would have saved them an awful lot of money."

Frontier Airlines claims to be the first to fly a known *stretched* aircraft. It was none other than "the Grand Ol' Lady" aircraft number 376. This all came about in the early days of Challenger Airlines (predecessor to Frontier). Chief pilot Scott Keller and senior pilot Bill McChrystal, two of the line's original pilots, were checking out the latest C-47/DC-3 they had taken delivery on. The chief suddenly became very excited and exclaimed that he had flown this very DC-3 when it had been assigned to the Troop Carrier Command. Captain McChrystal asked him how he could know that. The chief replied, "Because of the serial number, and it's stretched from the gliders loaded with troops I towed over the channel." Aircraft 376 was actually six inches longer than the rest of the fleet. So Frontier Airlines had the distinction of flying a stretched aircraft long before those prodigies came up with the idea.

Of special interest, this same aircraft had followed the chief around the world. Keller flew aircraft 19542 (376) while stationed at the 308th Troop Carrier Squadron at George Field, Illinois in 1943. Later he was assigned to the 61st Troop Carrier Command attached to the 9th Air Force in England. Waiting for him upon his arrival was aircraft 19542, a pleasant surprise. This was the same aircraft that Keller and McChrystal were inspecting, only now it was designated aircraft N53376. Frontier Airlines kept 376 in service for 23 years with the name *Sunliner Wyoming*. After 376 was retired from Frontier, it ended up serving with Air Manila in the Philippines only to meet a sad fate. While parked on the ramp, it was destroyed by a typhoon in 1970.

As a youth, the dreams and desires of Captain Keller was to fly. With the approach of WWII while attending college he joined the aviation cadet program in 1941. He won his wings and was commissioned in 1942 at Ellington Airfield, Houston, Texas. Retiring from the airlines because of the age sixty requirement, Captain Keller continued flying corporate jets and still does. Now known as the ancient pelican, Keller resides near the shore of the beautiful Flathead Lake in Lakeside, Montana.

33

Tribulations

A favorite story the copilots of many airlines loved to tell has been repeated for generations. An aircraft from one of our major carriers was on approach to the runway when the captain suddenly slumped over. The copilot immediately assumed command and safely landed the aircraft. Later, in the crew room, a captain was overheard to say, "I didn't know we had any copilots who knew how to land an airplane." From the back of the room, a copilot loudly asserted, "I wonder how that copilot knew the captain was dead."

Two chief pilots were taking their annual simulator check at the same time. Everything was normal in the Prop Jet 580 simulator until the left engine flamed out. The chief pilot, flying from the left seat, called to his cohort who was acting copilot, "Feather the right engine." Doing as ordered, the chief pilot in the right seat shut the right engine down.

With both engines shut down, there was a moment of complete silence until the simulator instructor informed the chief pilot in the left seat that he had instructed his cohort to shut down the right engine. He then explained it was the left engine that was the problem.

The chief pilot hollered, "The hell I gave the wrong order. I told him to shut the right engine down and he shut the wrong engine down."

"There are No Old Bold Pilots"

After the aircraft had pulled up to the chocks, the captain hurried aft to occupy the blue room. While comfortably seated there, the door suddenly opened. There stood the stew with an elderly lady she was trying to help. Seeing the captain had already laid claim to the throne, the stew became flustered, and turning to the lady, began introducing her to the captain. The captain, a gentleman, interrupted, "You'll pardon me if I don't stand." Never again did the captain forget to latch the door lock.

In 1958 a former Air Force general named Elwood R. Quesada was named the new FAA Administrator to replace the old Civil Aeronautics Administration. Quesada was demanding, had a short temper, and was determined to shape up the airlines. One of his first orders: FAA inspectors riding on jets began holding stopwatches on captains when they entered the blue room—six minutes was the time limit. This edict caused quite a stink among crewmembers in the cockpit, and was the reason many crewmembers raced to the blue room after landing.

The author flew with a copilot who had been domiciled in Dallas, Texas, and he told about his father who was a retired American Airlines captain. One time his dad was in the latter stages of his simulator check, making a partial panel approach (an approach using a minimum of flight instruments) with one engine shut down and several components of the instrument landing system inoperative. He was already fatigued from having flown the night before, and felt somewhat crotchety. He advised the simulator instructor, "This may not be purty, but I'll get her on the ground in one piece."

About this time the FAA inspectors walked in to observe, as they sometimes do. Not aware of all the problems the captain was trying to overcome, one inspector advised, "You're not making this approach according to the book."

From the side of his mouth, the captain shot back, "Who in hell said I was flying this approach by the book?"

Feeling unwelcome around this old line captain, whom they could not intimidate, the inspectors turned and quietly left.

The Plumed Bird

Competition among airlines to increase their load factors has resulted in many schemes to attract the traveling public's business. Among such was fare cutting, champagne flights, better food service, more leg room, upgraded equipment, and better scheduling. As previously mentioned, Braniff International Airlines went even further. They came up with an incredible scheme of painting their fleet with different eye-catching shades of blues and oranges with gaudy greens. Some I liked; others looked like they may have overshot the runway and splattered into a paint store. It seemed to serve its purpose—Braniff reported it increased their revenue by eighteen percent.

I was dead-heading in the cockpit of one of Braniff's painted DC-8s to Denver from Dallas. From what the crew told me, this plane was used on their routes to South America. Braniff had paid Alexander Calder, the famous American sculptor, $100,000 to design a paint scheme for this DC-8. I was riding in the world's first flying work of art. I guess it looked all right to art lovers, but to me it looked like it had been painted with whatever was available from partly emptied paint cans. It resembled a South American bird noted for the brilliance of its red, blue, yellow, and white plumage. The adornment of unknown illustrated configurations on the white engine nacelles reminded me of South American embellishments. But who am I to judge art? This abstract masterwork of Calder's not only repaid Braniff's cash investment, it also earned them tremendous amounts of publicity. The crew informed me however, that there *was* a problem. Parrots came out of the jungle and tried to make love to it.

A flushed stew rushed into the cockpit and told Captain Seymour Isaacs that there was a passenger in the blue room smoking marijuana. "I've demanded he stop smoking and unlock the blue room door, but he just ignores me," she said. She told the captain he better damn well do something about it. Captain Isaacs reached up and turned the *No Smoking* sign on.

Know What I Mean?

Then there is the old boomer pilot. He may be one of those who fell to the wayside as a young pilot, or his ambition may have been to boom from one flying job to another, never graduating to the cockpit of a scheduled airline. The day comes quickly when he discovers age has ascended upon him and the ever attending need for that one more flight arrives. One of the old boomers from many years back told how it was with him.

"You airline folks made the right decision in working for an airline. You even got to fly a Dizzy Three. Hell, you lasted thirty years flyin' for one outfit that had expert folks in the fix 'em up department, and you flew all over the U.S. and Canada and Mexico, too. Besides gettin' paid for that, you got a pension when you got old. Know what I mean?

"Hell, I ain't got nothin'. I've worked for a passel of charter outfits. If I found one of 'em that maintained their equipment, and the pay was good, hell, I thought I'd died and gone to heaven on an updraft. But they were few and far between. Those outfits that could cut the mustard were bought out by bigger outfits, or crashed in bankruptcy from all the make-a-quick-buck charter compilations. I was always left out there standin' on the ramp wondern' if one of those compilations across the way could use a good ol' boy, who needs just one more flight. Know what I mean?

"One outfit I worked for was tight with the bucks. They'd send a bottle of bargain whiskey on each flight. After leveling off at cruise altitude, the normal procedure was for me to announce happy hour had arrived, then pull the cork and pass the bottle around. Know what I mean?

"Another old red–nosed captain I was far-fetched to fly with changed the procedure. After takeoff he would holler, 'gear up and cork out.' When he leveled off at cruise altitude, he was flying high and the plane was flying low and there was nothin' left for happy hour.

"I can't vouch for this, but I think most of the other pilots consumed the contents themselves to keep their flying courage up. I know that at the end of the flight, the landing gear on those ol' boys looked pretty wobbly as they navigated across the ramp. Know what I mean?

"A finked-out passenger commented that the examining physician who had given those poor overworked boomers a clean bill of health on their medical certificate should be sued for malpractice. One mechanic who claimed he worked for Overcast Airlines related it was his duty to drive down the runway in a pickup truck after each departing flight to pick up the parts that had fallen off the aircraft. I wanted to quit when I heard this but hell, I needed the money. I guess I'll end up just like that old trail hand who kept riding 'til he fell off his horse, dead. They stuck him in a hole and left him. Hell, all that's out there now is a memory. The coyotes ate the real thing. Know what I mean?"

Those old boomers will keep right on vocalizing even after you find it necessary to leave. If you glance over your shoulder you'll find them still waving their arms and hollering, know what I mean?

There will always be stories to listen to and pass on, by old retired pilots whose memories keep their spirits soaring. But the best memory of all was time spent in the left seat.

This story comes from a friend who said his brother had a friend who had an uncle who told of an old retired airline pilot who wouldn't stay grounded, so he bought and flew his own light plane. Pushing eighty years old the pilot wouldn't face the fact that his eyesight had become lame and he had lost his depth perception. The FAA examining physician did him a favor by pulling his ticket. His chances of flaring out at a proper height above the runway while landing were about as good as a blind prospector striking gold while digging in a dung hill.

He said, "I would have been all right, because I took my wife along on every flight."

"If she doesn't know how to fly," his friend asked, "what is the purpose of that?"

"When I'm descending to the runway for a landing, I wait until she screams, then I haul back on the yoke and flair for the touchdown."

34

Professionals

Pilots these days are considered by many to be glorified truck drivers who keep watch over hi-tech contrivances and remonstrate because they have to fly an old Boeing 707 or a 737-200 instead of a gleaming new 757 or 767. Just the same, you can rest assured the captain climbing into the cockpit of his polished marvel to begin his run is thoroughly qualified in all aspects to conduct that flight. He has demonstrated his skills to Federal Aviation Examiners for the various ratings he is required to obtain. He has attended schools on every subject to meet those standards. He has been trained to know and understand the various weather patterns he may encounter in his career. Before each flight he studies all the latest weather charts for his route and is aware of the actual weather conditions forecast to be encountered.

He has studied and flown thousands of hours to climb the ladder of required ratings to qualify for that final step: the Airline Transport Rating.

Today, as you see the captain enter the cockpit, be assured that in times past he has flown copilot with captains who took him under their wing, and from their years of experience, imparted valuable knowledge and training. Through the years he has changed from a fledgling to a respected eagle.

He has completed specialized courses for the type of aircraft he will be flying this day. He thoroughly understands all the flight procedures for this particular aircraft. He is knowledgeable and understands the operation of the various systems, as well as the backup systems. He understands the emergency procedures for unexpected problems, and is tested with oral and written examinations. He is required to demonstrate his skills in all phases of flight, including emergencies and weather-related problems. Upon a successful completion he is awarded a Type Rating Certificate for the aircraft you are boarding.

It is an ongoing requirement that he demonstrate his skills every six months in the simulator to qualified check FAA airmen with a review on systems and flight procedures. During the climb to the top rung of the ladder, several hundred thousands of dollars have been consumed to qualify him for that left-seat authority. During his career he will accumulate thousands of hours of experience flying the line. Experience is still the principal mentor and every flight is a learning experience.

He is required to know all the Federal Regulations pertaining to the profession and interpret them into airman's jargon. An airline pilot is the most regulated mortal on the face of the earth.

A well-trained flight crew has to accomplish an exact set of procedures to bring a turn of events caused by a malfunctioning component to a successful conclusion. The following incident report written thirty years ago by First Officer Gary A. Winn is a good example.

Captain Gary A. Winn: *On the morning of September 8, 1967 we were flying flight 504, a prop jet Convair 580 into Riverton, Wyoming. On the approach everything was routine. Captain Bagshaw called for gear down and the final checklist. We observed the transit light was still on and only two green lights, one for the nose and one for the left main gear, were indicating. The right main gear light was not indicating green. Captain Bagshaw asked me to make a positive check by depressing a micro switch on the pedestal (a position indicator on the right gear), but the results were negative. We discontinued the approach and initiated a go-around.*

We requested inbound flight 503, who was arriving in the area, to fly alongside and make a visual inspection of the gear. They confirmed the right main gear was still in its well, and the gear doors had not opened. The gear handle was cycled several times but the condition persisted. I flew the aircraft while the captain followed the procedure from the flight manual for "blowing" the gear up-latches. The results were negative as indicated by the lights and confirmed by flight 503. The stewardess and passengers were then advised of the situation.

After conversing with the dispatchers in Denver, it was determined the flight should continue to Denver where better equipment was available to handle a variety of problems. An amended clearance was issued and the flight was cleared direct to Denver via radar vector at an altitude of 17,000 feet. En route, the procedures for gear up landings were reviewed and all loose equipment in the aircraft was properly stowed.

Arriving over Denver at 10:00 a.m., the tower and company dispatch operated on the same frequency to expedite communications. Until the final decision was made to bellyland the aircraft, we tried almost every conceivable configuration to release the up-latches. Positive Gs and negative Gs were applied to the aircraft in an attempt to break the gear free. During these maneuvers we actuated the gear handle up and down with no success.

We tried several more applications from the emergency air bottle to blow the up-latches with no success. Seeking every available resource to solve the problem, the left engine was shut down to release the hydraulic pressure on the up-latches, but with no success.

With the fuel down to 1,600 pounds, a decision was made to bellyland the aircraft. Runway 17 was foamed while the captain went to the cabin to once again reassure the passengers and inform them of the decision to land with all the gear up. He told them the last thing before landing would be the removal of the emergency window exits. The stewardess completed the procedures for preparing the passengers, who were ready and seemed reasonably calm.

Turning a long final for runway 17 and following the captain's commands, I dumped the pressurization. The emergency exit windows in the passenger cabin were removed and stored. The captain and I again reviewed the final procedures. Flaps were set at 28 degrees, an airspeed of 120 knots was maintained. At 1,000 feet from the runway the alternators and inverter switches were positioned off. I continually called out the airspeed and altitude, and placed both my hands on the E handles (emergency handles). At approximately 50 feet above the field elevation Captain Bagshaw gave the order: "E handles now." The E handle for each engine feathers the large propellers and shuts off the supply of oil, fuel, and hydraulic fluid. In the same motion the overhead fuel tank switches and emergency power switches were turned off and, lastly, the master power switch was positioned off. During the remaining 50 feet of decreasing altitude, Captain Bagshaw was flying a powerless aircraft to a dead stick landing.

In Captain Bagshaw's own words he said, "I then concentrated on flying the aircraft to the center line of the foam. Touchdown was made softly onto the foam. No great deceleration was noticed until after the foam ended, after which a rocking motion was felt until coming to a standstill. I looked back and yelled 'let's go.' I saw two men exiting through the exit windows on the right side, and the rest exited through the rear service door except for one elderly lady who was still sitting in her seat. I helped her to the rear exit where two passengers were standing and assisting everyone out. I checked back through the cabin and no one was inside except First Officer Winn. We jumped out with assistance from the two passengers and we all departed the immediate area."

The crew was highly praised for their professional handling of the incident, and that's what they are, professionals.

A little background on the pilots involved in this incident. Captain B. B. Bagshaw served in the U.S. Air Force as a fighter pilot. He flew the F86, and then was chosen to fly the North American F100 Super Sabre, the first second lieutenant to do so. The Super Sabre was the world's first supersonic fighter, with a top speed of 910 mph, it was the first jet to exceed the speed of sound in level flight. It incorporated heat-resistant titanium alloys. It had a 1,060 mile range that could be extended via in-flight refueling. Bob was the highest time F-100 pilot in the Air Force when he separated from the service.

Captain Bagshaw flew many of the large jet transports in his career as an airline pilot. He served two years as a first officer with Trans World Airlines. He flew the Martin 404, and all models of the beautiful Lockheed Constellation. Wanting to be based in the west, he joined Frontier in 1958. After the demise of Frontier, he served with a number of airlines in the capacity of captain, simulator instructor and check airman. He is rated on the DC-3, CV-580, MD-80, B-737, B-727, B-707, and B-720. At the present time he is working in the training program with Win Air based in Salt Lake City.

First officer Gary Winn followed his father's footsteps. He flew a variety of aircraft in his military career, including both the cargo and the refueling versions of the C-97 which were offspring of the famous B-29. He also flew the C-47, and "old shaky," the huge Douglas-built C-124 Globe Master. The Lockheed T33 he flew was a version of America's first jet fighter, the F-80 Shooting Star.

Captain Winn, like Captain Bagshaw, went on to fly large passenger jets. After Frontier Airlines was brought to the ground for the last time, Captain Gary Winn continued working in the training program of a number of airlines, and currently is a simulator instructor and check airman with Win Air in Salt Lake City. He is the son of General Alma Winn who was active in the military for thirty-eight years. General Winn first learned to fly in 1936. One of General Winn's assignments was base commander of the large Hill Field Air Base in Utah for two years after WWII, and then he headed up the Utah National Guard until his retirement in 1967.

35

All in a Day's Work

Captain Billy Walker tells his story now:

I was flying a CV-580 from Denver to West Yellowstone through Jackson Hole then back to Denver on June 6, 1979. We had a full load of passengers and two mechanics on board, one of which was on the jump seat while the other occupied a seat in the cabin. The mechanics were going to Jackson to repair another CV-580 that had a mechanical problem.

Other than heavy clouds with some airframe icing, the flight was pretty much uneventful from Denver to West Yellowstone. However, descending into West Yellowstone, the compressor light flickered on and off. I asked the mechanic if he would mind servicing the compressor when we arrived in Jackson. No problem.

It was the copilot's leg, WYS-JAC, with everything normal up to our level-off at flight level 180 (18,000 feet). Then the compressor light illuminated steady and the decision was made to disconnect the compressor per Frontier's procedures. We had to descend to the minimum enroute altitude of 11,300 feet so the passengers would have a comfortable supply of oxygen. On the descent and at the minimum enroute altitude, we encountered quite a bit of rime ice (keep in mind this is on June 6th). Naturally, I selected the de/anti-icing. However, the left side wing anti-ice would not activate. The essential bus was behind the captain's head where certain circuit breakers could be re-set to activate stubborn systems. We did this, albeit to no avail.

Soon we were turning the corner to intercept the Jackson Instrument Landing System when the fire warning bell activated without fire warning lights. I had the mechanic reach over and silence the bell, then turn it back on only to have the bell continue ringing without fire warning lights. I had the copilot check to see if the starter arm switch was accidentally bumped on. It wasn't. Then I had the mechanic reset the fire bell switch and with the bell ringing, I pressed the fire test and the number two engine wheelwell light illuminated and stayed on. After a retest, the light still remained on. Now we were unpressurized, with a fair buildup of ice on our left wing and (presumably) our tail, along with indications telling us we had an engine fire. Of course we elected to follow the procedures and went through the engine fire checklist. Since the wheelwell was presumably on fire and, remembering a previous incident with the CV-340 years before, I elected to put the gear down early in hopes the tires were not on fire too.

I called Jackson to check the weather while the copilot, Jeff Benger, did a beautiful job flying the ILS in solid IFR. With our unusual icing dilemma, Jackson gave me the bad news that the airport was below minimums with slush on the runway and a crosswind from the left at fifteen knots gusting to twenty.

I called the flight attendant up front and asked her to relay a message to the mechanic in back to inspect the number 2 engine and for him to pay especially close attention to the tailpipe and the wheels as those were viewable from his position in the cabin.

The fire light didn't go out after firing the first bottle, and the bottle supply light would not illuminate even though it tested properly. So, I fired the second bottle. No luck! The supply light would not illuminate other than the push-to-test and the fire light stayed illuminated along with the bell (if the switch was left on).

I assumed control of the aircraft as I needed to get on the nose steering upon landing while the copilot maintained aileron control deflection and forward yoke. With the number two engine shut down, a left-hand crosswind, along with deteriorating runway conditions we had our work cut out for us. Jeff then continued reading the checklists. Every once in a while I would look back at the mechanic thinking it must be Elmer Burson (deceased simulator instructor) famous for his malfunctions in the simulator back there causing all this (grin). But, alas it was the mechanic who had been on the jump seat from Denver. He had little beady eyes when we left Denver and now they were about the size of a saucer! He made every effort to be helpful, but the airplane was uncooperative.

The second mechanic riding in the cabin came forward to report the mist from freezing rain and clouds was too dense to see much, but he could just make out the tires that looked normal.

As the copilot checked the items off he started to relay to me the missed-approach procedures. I said there will not be a go-around. The condition of the aircraft coupled with the weather and terrain considerations would not allow this and I was determined to take the safest approach which was to get us on the runway safely even if conditions were zero-zero.

We radioed to have the emergency crew posted at the approach end of the runway and for them to try to see if there was any evidence of fire. If there was evidence of fire, we would immediately evacuate the aircraft on the runway. Our flight attendant, Sally Douglas, stepped into the cockpit to report she had the cabin prepared for an emergency evacuation and would wait for any announcement from us after touchdown. Like all of our flight attendants, she is a real professional and did a fantastic job considering where we were and the number of people on board (54 including crew and the additional crewmember).

We broke out around 150 feet. Slush makes for a nice touchdown, but really squirrelly on the runway with the direct crosswind. With a thumbs up from the ground crew, I elected to taxi to the ramp. For only a 26-minute scheduled leg we had been busy. The amazing part is having a mechanic on the jump seat observing all this. Interestingly, there was actually little wrong with the airplane. The fire bottles did fire, a fact we could have discerned from our flight attendant as they scared the pants off her. She said it sounded like a cannon. The bottles are in the belly under her seat! Later we found that the switch where the bottles were located was defective and would not pop up to turn on the supply light.

The fire sensor loop was at fault and that caused the fire warning to ring. The compressor did need service and the anti-ice valves needed adjustment too.

I would shut down the engine again if facing the same situation because there was no way we could know for sure if we had a fire with the compounded situation we were facing. I guess that's what procedures are for.

The mechanic that was on the jump seat said he would remain on the ground from then on and fix airplanes with both his feet planted on solid earth. I still wonder if his saucer-sized eyes ever returned to normal. As for me, I still wonder if that old simulator instructor Elmer Burson had something to do with all that.

Tex, I would have given anything in this world to have finished my career with good ol' Frontier. When I allow myself to look back, it is through tear-filled eyes. They say we should never look back, but how can you not think *about the close relationship we had on Frontier. It was there, and I'm glad I got to be a part of it. Those were the golden years of flying for me.*

Today, Captain Walker manages the A320 Fleet Training for America West Airlines. Additionally, he is a check pilot and a Federal Aviation Administration examiner. For recreation he is finishing a ⅞ scale replica WWI Nieuport 17 fighter, and will fly with several others in the Lafayette Escadrille de Arizona 17 Squadron.

Captain Walker's mother, Frances Emily Walker, was the first woman to learn to fly in Wyoming in the 1930s. Knowing his father, Pic Walker, was an Elder Statesman of Aviation, and being somewhat familiar with Pic's history, I would like to relate some of his background.

In 1924 Pic flew the long-winged OX-5 powered Alexander Eaglerock. He did some barnstorming and later operated three CPT (Civilian Pilot Training) flight schools for the U.S. Army. He was posthumously inducted into the Wyoming Aviation Hall of Fame as the first to be selected. He was named Elder Statesman of Aviation by the National Aeronautic Association. His life went from that of a six-year-old kid riding on a stage coach from Meeker, to Rifle, Colorado, to that of seeing men walk on the moon.

At the time of the CPT program, Dave Cannon (who later flew as a Frontier line captain) was the Army Air Corps liaison officer and became good friends with Pic and his wife. Captain Cannon, as a matter of fact, used to change the diapers of young Billy. Fact is stranger than fiction, because in later years, young Billy became a first officer on Frontier and flew many copilot trips with Captain Dave Cannon. Billy acknowledges that Captain Cannon liked to embarrass him when the young stewardesses were around with the bit of trivia about changing his diapers.

36

Women in the Cockpit

On one of my last trips for the airline, I checked the manifest. The passenger count was correct, the total weight added up correctly, the lights indicated all the doors were secured, and we were cleared to spool the engines. After startup we received the all-clear from ground personnel to depart the gate. I opened the clamshells to reverse the direction of the thrust and slowly backed the Boeing until clear of the jetway. After completing the before-taxi checklist, the first officer requested clearance to taxi. A female voice cleared us to the active runway. The before-takeoff checklist was completed and we were ready to smoke the wild blue yonder. The copilot changed over to the tower frequency and requested clearance for takeoff. A female voice cleared us for takeoff, and to contact departure control after we were off the ground. The copilot made the comment, "What is this world coming to?"

Someone answered, "You haven't heard the last of it yet." Changing over to departure control, the copilot reported in. Another female; this one said she had us on radar and she monitored our flight until we were asked to call the enroute traffic controllers. Before switching frequencies the copilot remarked, "Were they all really female controllers? Maybe they're male controllers who had their seat belts fastened too tight?"

More women are making a career in aviation than ever, and they are doing an excellent job. Frontier Airlines hired the first female pilot in the United States, Emily Howell Warner, to fly for a regularly scheduled airline. Although it was never my privilege to fly the line with her, she did fly copilot for me on a simulator check, and she did an exceptional job. I heard that before coming on the line in 1973 she had served as a flight instructor and had even instructed several of our copilots.

The following information was taken from an article ("America's First Female Airline Pilot") in *Arizona Flyways* by former Frontier Captain Billy Walker:

> *Between 1973 and 1986 Emily would fly as first officer and captain on the DHC-6, Convair 580, and the Boeing 737. She also became the first female captain; and in 1986 Emily would command the first all-female flight crew for a scheduled airline in the United States. Captain Warner has been honored nationally and internationally. She has logged 21,000 total flight hours, and 14,000 of that as an airline pilot. Now as an FAA aviation safety inspector, she is an air crew program manager and is assigned to the United Airlines Boeing 737 fleet.*

As Captain Walker said in the *Arizona Flyways* article, "Atta boy, girl!"

Old pilots were becoming a little confused by female pilots in the cockpit and male flight attendants serving in the cabin. Their mind-set remained in a state of bafflement with this placement of the new generation of flight crews.

Most Accomplished Aviatrix

Over the years many cockpit crews have expressed their opinions (some heated) about who was the most accomplished aviatrix. These discourses linger on with many opinions being expressed. The hangar dialogue can sometimes be a little assertive, so in resurrecting asserted opinions for the world's finest female pilot, certain guidelines must prevail and the overall background should be considered. It is not how famous an individual has become from a singular outstanding feat, but from a series of accomplishments. Achievements and performances all combined together to make that pilot outstanding.

Looking back over the years at the number of women involved in aviation, many have accomplished daring feats still held in high esteem in the annals of aviation. Amelia Earhart was always a forerunner in many heated discussions. She gained fame as a long distance flyer and is probably the most noted, but to classify her as the best female pilot in this country? Her name was down the list.

The name Jackie Cochran was at the top of the list. Flying a Staggerwing Beechcraft, in 1937 she came in third in the Bendix contest, competing against a field of male pilots flying the fastest racing planes of that era. Then in 1938, again flying against a field of men, she won first place. She won many races and became known as the Speed Queen. She held the women's international speed record. She set a new women's altitude record, and became the first woman to make a blind landing. She was the first female to fly a bomber across the Atlantic. She headed up the WASP program during WWII. She flew the dangerous Gee Bee R-2, a very unstable racer that killed several pilots. You might say she flew everything from Cubs to B-29s. As a skilled pilot her technique was impeccable.

She also flew many jet fighters including the F-104 that killed many Luftwaffe pilots. She logged over 15,000 hours and has flown at speeds of over 1,500 mph. Yes, the feeling prevailed that Jackie Cochran is this country's best female pilot ever.

Not well known in this country is Germany's Hanna Reitsch. She learned to fly gliders in 1931. She attended the all-male Civil Airways Training School. With her gifted skills she soon distinguished herself as a remarkable pilot and was chosen as a test pilot for the Luftwaffe. She test flew the Fa-61 helicopter in 1937, a craft with twin rotors that was very unstable. She test flew about every plane Germany developed. She flew them all from gliders to seaplanes, fighters, and bombers.

As one of Germany's top test pilots she was chosen to test fly the radical Me 163B rocket plane in 1942. Looking at photographs of the Komet in flight without a horizontal tail reminded one of a moth. It was only a little over 18 feet long, with a wingspan of 30 feet, 8 inches, a rocket plane way ahead of its time. Unfortunately for Germany, the aircraft that was designed to stop the onslaught of allied bombers in WWII killed more of its own than enemy pilots.

They were especially dangerous on the ground. It was propelled by rocket propellants and if the takeoff roll was rough and the two propellants accidentally came together, it would explode. It was sometimes referred to as the chemical cocktail. It had no landing gear, and took off on a specially designed, wheeled trolley cart that was released after take off. It climbed at a steep angle to high altitudes with speeds approaching 600 mph, a remarkable performance in those days. With the propellants consumed, it would dive at high speeds on the bomber formations. Gliding in for a landing was a one-shot approach. For landing, it utilized a skid. Hanna Reitsch suffered near-fatal injuries in a Messerschmitt 163 Komet after she was compelled to make a forced landing with a flawed wheel trolley hang up.

She continued on to test fly the V-1 bomb that was specially fitted with a cockpit, and launched from a bomber. After its perfection it was a pilotless flying bomb, sometimes referred to as the buzz bomb by the British on hearing its dreaded buzzing in the skies over London. Its wide-ranging devastation was catastrophic.

Hanna Reitsch was the only woman awarded the Iron Cross First Class for her achievements, talented skills, and her many contributions to aviation. After WWII, she was compelled to hand over all her pilot credentials and was never allowed to fly as a test pilot again. She passed away in 1979. From expressed dialogue of the past, I would unequivocally name Hanna Reitsch as the world's most gifted female pilot.

37

After Retirement

When a dedicated airline pilot turns in the key to the cockpit and takes that long walk to sign out for the last time, as required by the age sixty mandate, his emotions on a scale of one to ten are about a baker's dozen. Emotions generated by a long career that is by now embedded in his soul. Some pilots handle it well, even look forward to retirement. Some, even though they have attempted to prepare for this momentous change in lifestyle, make poor pretense in facing reality. But every one of them is grateful for having had the ride.

When you think back to when every youngster wanted to drive a fire engine or run a train or fly an airplane, you are aware that while many never lost those desires and dreams, few ever reached them. If a young man's life's ambition is to fly for an airline, then he faces a hard, long row to meet this challenge. How to obtain that goal is a decision only he can determine. Some are fortunate enough to receive their flight training through the military, but this door is open only to the select few needed to fill the peace time requirements of the Navy and Air Force quotas.

If he decides to accomplish his goal through general aviation schools in the private sector, he must be prepared to shell out a large amount of money to obtain the required ratings. Somehow he must complete the minimum requirement of two years of college, while knowing that four years will increase the odds of a second look at his resume. Then he must prepare to seek employment with a commuter affiliate or charter carrier or one of the many commercial operators to build his flying hours to the minimum specified time required by the major carrier he is seeking employment with. Obtaining the coveted Airline Transport Pilot Certificate places him on an even keel with the master degree possessor. Even this does not guarantee employment, but may help in getting him through the door for that all-important interview.

If luck is with him and he receives notification of a hiring date to begin training, he has hurdled the first step in a career full of never-ending study and testing.

Achieving these goals, he can now reap the reward of proudly sitting in the *right* seat and becoming part of the team. An old pilot, satisfied that he made the right choices, remembers all the hurdles on the way to the *left* seat and wonders where the time went. Fortunate indeed is the man doing exactly what he likes to do. The years swiftly fly when the task is enjoyable. Too swiftly. Then, abruptly and recklessly, the careers of veteran pilots are interrupted by the swipe of a pen, because of the age 60 rule implemented by a bureaucratic FAA without a public hearing or any credible evidence that a pilot who is healthy one day is a detriment the next day.

An old pilot scanning over his logbooks is always amazed at the many types of aircraft he has flown, and at how few passengers he carried in the beginning compared to the hundreds that now occupy the cabin. He witnessed the enormous growth of an industry made possible by the bursting progress of advanced technology. He remembers when the nosewheel was the tailwheel and a smooth takeoff and landing were challenges to be mastered, something a pilot could really be proud of. He'll always carry the thrill of accomplishment in shooting tight approaches in inclement weather, and remembering the many friends made over years of shared camaraderie will always be uplifting.

Occasionally a retired pilot will rev up his soul by taking memory flights over his favorite routes—to Mexico, for example, during the winter to land in the brilliant sunshine and enjoy the friendly chatter of the Mexican people. Or to Phoenix, Arizona, before the day of the jetway and tight security measures, to step onto the ramp in the springtime and enjoy the fragrance of orange blossoms in bloom. (If the breezes flowed from the other direction, the scent from the stockyards presented a little nostalgia to a farm boy.) Life is like the wind—exhilarating and melancholy. An observant pilot will replenish his soul with the sweet life to bind him over for when the ill winds blow.

Many pilots in retirement gather together for meetings or luncheons and reminisce about good times in the sky. It is a pleasant time to hangar talk of the early years when flying was down to earth. As one old time mail pilot said, "How can they have any fun these days, flying way up there in the sky."[11]

38

Flying for the Nonscheds

Many airline pilots, not wanting to stay grounded after forced retirement, elect to work for charter outfits or mail contractors or fly for corporations. Some even go so far as to work for the FAA. Flying under Part 135 (less restrictive air regulations) these operators do not come under the age restriction the scheduled airlines have inherited.

Like many pilots, I thought of the alternatives to get me back in the air. In checking out Majestic Air, I found they were flying the Grand Ol' Lady, the beautiful Learjet, Beech 18s, the classy Beechcraft Turbo Baron, and the Aero Commander with its 340-hp engines. I hired on with Majestic Air as the Director of Training and as a check pilot. Then I soon found myself flying mail runs in DC-3s and Beech 18s. It was like going back in time to the 1930s and 1940s. Yes, I was in my second childhood and living my dream. Later, I found myself serving as chief pilot, a position I disdained. I wanted to fly more.

Two retired airline pilots, Captains Al Kendell and Captain Seymour Isaacs, were already aboard. Along the way two other retired airline pilots came aboard, Captain Jack Schade and Captain Ron Rasmussen. I overheard a comment made by one of our young pilots, "Those old aeronauts are so old, they don't know they're old." We felt like we had been resurrected from ground zero and boosted up from the face of the earth. Except for the Learjet, the equipment wasn't swift, but it kept us in the air.

Flying the war surplus Twin Beech F-2 on the mail run from Salt Lake City to Billings, Montana in the winter isn't to every pilot's liking. Short of help on a cold January morning, I crawl into the small cockpit and crank up the two 450-hp Pratt & Whitney Wasp Jr. engines. Heavy with a load of mail I climb into the low hanging clouds.

Flying at 13,000 feet I have occasional light ice. The propeller anti-icing system is working well to prevent ice buildup on the props. The incoming heated airflow in the cockpit makes for a cozy atmosphere. Flying encompassed in a sea of clouds is like flying inside a large ping-pong ball. The continuous sea of gray clouds engulf me on my route of flight, but, this is my calling and I am confined in a familiar setting where I have spent several years of my life.

The two Pratt & Whitney Wasp Jrs have a pow pow resonance, and I know they are singing this melody just for me. I no longer need the airlines that are steeped in modernity. I'm flying an aircraft that is over 50 years old. I'm looking at an instrument panel that has the bare necessities for instrument flight. I'm listening to engines that sound like aircraft engines should sound. I'm flying the mail and all I need is a helmet with goggles and a scarf. Well, maybe I don't need the goggles and helmet, because I'd look sort of ridiculous sitting in an enclosed cockpit wearing that outfit. Maybe when no one is looking...

The turbulence is warning the F-2 that she'll be picking up more ice shortly, and with the manifold pressure decreasing and the airspeed falling off, she's telling me that carburetor ice is choking her. I need to get heat into those dudes now. What's that fracas? The propellers are slinging ice. Sorry ol' gal, I'll feed the slinger rings a little more juice to fortify your props and actuate your wing leading edge boots so you can shed the wing ice. The outside temperature gauge says we're in the best range for picking up demon ice. If we go lower we're going to find rocks in these clouds. The old F-2 is beginning to shudder; she's on the verge of a stall and is refusing to climb.

She's got full power and is still complaining. Got to get more heat into the carburetors despite the reduction in needed power it causes. She keeps asking for every fraction of power the Wasp Jrs can muster, and at the same time she insists I keep heat flowing into her carburetors to free up the carb-ice or she's gonna shut down. It's a trade off: carburetor heat on and the power drops off—carburetor heat off and the power returns to normal. But then she stuffs more ice into her carburetors and again the power falls off and the airspeed decreases. How long can I keep trading power for heat? She's accumulating all the wing ice the Wyoming skies can harvest. She knows she can't out-duel Mother Nature, but she's trying. Do this—do that! Besides being a bit contrary, she's acting crazy. What do I have to do to make her happy? Now the throttle levers won't budge, she wants carburetor alcohol crammed into those dude's immediately or her disposition is going to deteriorate even more. If that happens she's going to trash the Wyoming countryside and I want no part of it.

Whose calling me on the other radio? You say my microphone button is stuck? Can't you folks see I'm busy?

You want a weather report? It's a duel between the Beech and Mother Nature, and the odds are on Mother Nature. I'll call you back.

Did you say I can have a lower altitude if I need it? I need it, and I'm starting down now.

Why is it so cold in here? The damn heater has mutinied.

Get the Billings approach plates out. I guess I'm talking to myself, there's no copilot on this trip.

Ah! I'm out the bottom, and I can see the Billings airport. Sweet salvation.

I can't feel the rudder pedals with my feet. I can't even feel my feet. I wonder if Billings can repair the heater?

Pretty good landing for a frozen-legged ol' pilot.

Unless I quit talking to myself when the mike is keyed open, those controllers will think they're talking to an old man.

What's that you asked? How was my flight? Just a piece of cake.

Over the many years of flying the environment, I've thought about those people who claimed to have conquered the seas or the air. To me, that was just talk. We have never conquered any of the elements. Sometimes tremendous feats have been accomplished in dealing with the elements, but that was usually when Mother Nature was looking the other way.

As one who loves the old prop jobs, I have to admit I will also be forever grateful to have flown the Learjet—every pilot's dream. We used it mainly to haul mail between Salt lake City and Denver. We would leave Salt Lake in the evening en route to Denver where we overnighted and arrive back in Salt Lake by eight o'clock the following morning. Twenty minutes later the Lear would be refueled and the interior changed back to the original executive interior with seven seats.

The Learjet 35

In departing Salt Lake City, the four or five doctors on board were transported to various cities throughout the west to set up clinics for the day for the Veterans Administration. We called it the VA run. During the day with nothing to do, Ron Rasmussen, my copilot and I would do a little sightseeing, then locate a good restaurant. Later, in the afternoon, he would pull out his banjo and crack me up with some of my old favorites. By evening the Lear would be back in Salt Lake City preparing for the next mail run to Denver.

Flying the Learjet at flight level 410 (41,000 feet) or above in the thin air gave me a feeling I was in another realm. I would look out the window at those small wings, and it would take some getting used to after the large transport type wing I had flown. It had one speed, and that was all out. To sharpen our skills, we would sometimes disconnect the autopilot and hand fly it at this thin density altitude. Being a heavy-handed transport pilot, I had to continually concentrate to maintain a constant altitude. But it did sharpen my awareness, and after a short time I was happy to re-engage the autopilot.

Captain Al Kendell and I flew the company Learjet to Tulsa from Salt Lake City for an engine hot-section change. Taking advantage of the smooth upper air, and to save fuel, we climbed through the troposphere to reach flight level 450 (45,000 feet) where we cruised nice and toasty in the subfreezing temperatures for over two hours. One hundred miles out from Tulsa we started our letdown. Tulsa was reporting temperatures in the high 80s with high humidity. As we descended into the warmer altitudes, the Lear taught us a lesson. Flying at flight level 450 for so long a time in subfreezing temperatures, the aircraft had become cold soaked.

The airflow defogging vents receiving forced warm air from the engine bleed air failed to remove the frosted humidity from inside the windshield. We tried to clear a see-through area with a wipe cloth. As we wiped furiously to rid the moisture, it returned behind the swathe faster than an old maid pursuing a marriage license.

I called, "Al! We can't see out."

He called back, "Anyone with a cork stuck in one eye, and a rag stuck in the other can see that."

Chuck Yeager had a similar problem with the Bell X-1. The problem was frost on the inside of his canopy also. Making a power-out gliding descent to Rogers Dry Lake, there was no way he could slow his descent until warmer temperatures eased some of his problem. As he continued a steep descent, Bob Hoover slid alongside the X-1 in the P-80 Shooting Star and talked Yeager down to a safe, blind landing.

Pilots flying the F-86 during the Korean conflict were always happy to see a MiG 15 turn tail and dive for the deck from 40,000 feet up. Knowing the MiG 15 had poor climate-control features, they would follow it down with the knowledge that when it descended to the warmer temperatures, the frost buildup on the inside of the canopy would restrict the pilot's outside vision and the MiG 15 would be history.

As the Lear descended into the warmer temperatures, we were able to eliminate enough of the frosty moisture to make out the runway and complete the landing. This problem was later eliminated with an add-on system.

Tailpipe Inspection

One of our maintenance personnel liked to tell the story of an FAA inspector who, in conducting a walk-around inspection of our Lear, always slipped a quarter into the tailpipe exhaust. Then, if the individual being tested failed to detect the quarter during the inspection, he was lectured on his careless walk-around performance.

One day, knowing this FAA inspector would be arriving shortly to conduct another walk-around inspection with a newly-hired applicant, the mechanics decided to have a little fun. After he had arrived with the applicant, the inspector slipped a quarter into the tailpipe. To divert the attention of the inspector, two mechanics started an argument on the other side of the Lear. When the inspector went to investigate the problem, another mechanic slipped over to the Lear and removed the quarter.

After the completion of the inspection, the FAA inspector started to chew the applicant out for not finding the quarter. He said, "If you had been a little more observant, you would have found a quarter lying in the exhaust pipe." The inspector reached his hand in to retrieve his quarter. Then drew back with a puzzled expression. In his hand were two dimes and a nickel.

While serving as chief pilot for Majestic Airlines, I was conducting a walk-around inspection for a newly-upgraded captain on the DC-3. One female student who had done well in the classroom and had completed her ground school requirements asked if she could observe. Everything was going well with the captain, who was answering all the questions. I thought I would quiz our observer on one of our more easily answered questions. I asked, "What type of engines do we have on our DC-3s?" Without hesitation she snapped, "Briggs & Stratton" (small lawn mower engine).

Shot Down at Elko, Nevada

Flying the DC-3 for Rocky Mountain Helicopter we were en route back to Provo, Utah after having delivered a load of helicopter parts to Klawock, Alaska, located on Prince of Wales Island. After landing at Boeing Field in Seattle to take on fuel, word came we were to be rerouted through Hayward, California to pick up a heavy helicopter transmission and several other components.

On the ground at Hayward, the cargo had been strapped down, and we departed eastbound for Provo. We climbed to our assigned altitude of 13,000 feet, and leaned back in our seats for the expected uneventful ride over a segment of this country's first transcontinental airmail route. Over Battle Mountain, Nevada, everything was as smooth as Chet's bread pudding when suddenly I felt a small vibration. Asking that the first officer scan his engine, I did the same out my window and it appeared to be reasonably smooth. When the first officer checked the engine cowling, he could make out a small vibration. About this time one of our helicopter mechanics from the cabin stepped into the cockpit and advised we had oil seepage at a good rate from the number two engine.

The oil pressure and temperature gauges indicated all was still normal, but knowing a gremlin had pulled the cork, and before he could empty the tank, I elected to shut down number two before it trashed itself. The Elko, Nevada airport lay about 40 miles ahead with clear skies, so I canceled the airways clearance with Oakland Center and called Elko radio. They reported wind out of the east which made it possible to land straight in on runway number 5.

After our arrival the mechanic immediately began troubleshooting the engine and soon discovered the problem. A scavenger oil return line had a hole in it. On closer inspection, he discovered that an unknown object had penetrated completely through the reinforced rubber hose, as a bullet would do. This brought back memories of a time when one of Frontier's DC-3s landed at Denver with a 30-06 caliber slug in it, put there by a deer hunter.

On further inspection, he detected a spark plug with a hollow interior. A Rocky Mountain maintenance inspector did a little research on the problem and found that on very rare occasions (1 in 5,000,000), a faulty spark plug has been known to erupt, blasting the interior workings out the end like a shot from a cannon. Only in my case this projectile penetrated an essential part of the oil system. Engineers have designed the radial engine with two spark plugs on each cylinder housing for extra protection against a malfunctioning plug. Now we need to design a plug that can't shoot straight.

This One Last Thought

In every pilot's career there comes a time when age requires him to make that final landing. He must turn in the keys to the front office and say farewell to a career that was full of wonderful things and places. He must say goodbye to the best pilots anyone could ever have had the good fortune to associate with. To you out there, wherever you may be, this one last thought I leave with you.

Our eyes are growing dim. Our hearing is impaired. Our time served in the air is over and we have come to the end of the runway. If I could have that one last wish, it would be to see and hear the resonance of a big Pratt & Whitney or Wright or even a Merlin singing its lovely melody just for you and me, high up there in the thin density air on a cold wintry day. The crisp, crystal-clear rhythmical movement is our symphony. Music from a chapter in life that is filed away forever. We were all fortune's children.

WAS IT ALL A DREAM?

Stepping from the cockpit for the last time, the reassuring words of Captain Bob Rich ring loudly in my ears.

"We were uniquely privileged to have participated in pioneering the art of flying the Rocky Mountains in a safe and reliable manner.

"Unquestionably, we needed the money. But as I have suggested, all seats arrive at the same time and we were very aware that everyone on the airplane was a soul for which we were responsible.

"Occasionally, you and I were subjected to extremely difficult situations. Our experience provided us with the moxie to depart A and arrive B intact.

"Fifty years later we can enjoy our families and grandchildren knowing that we did our best and it was damned good.

AN ENDING TO THE BEGINNING

Reclining in my favorite lounge chair, I continue to gaze into the tranquil sky, and I now see the wispy cirrus clouds with their mare's tails. I reminisce about it all. I miss the cobalt blue sunrises over the plains states of Kansas and Nebraska, and the fiery red sunsets in New Mexico. I miss the early morning silhouettes of majestic Rocky Mountain peaks pointing skyward, and flaming sunsets in the blue Pacific. I miss the moonlight on the Colorado River as it snakes its way out of the Rockies, and wharf lights glistening on the mighty Mississippi. I miss the millions of sparkling silhouettes urged on by soft breezes, as they skitter about on crested waves beckoning to a Great Salt Lake sunset. I especially miss the camaraderie of my fellow pilots and the sound of the big recips with their deep throb. I miss the smell of airplanes, and I miss touching them. I miss it all.

Hundreds of recip pilots who have sat across the pedestal from each other on a black night gazing into the star-filled heavens all share these memories. The greatness of an airline doesn't come from its large size, or all the updated equipment. It's the employees who make the best of what they have and dedicate their hearts and souls to making it work. That's what makes a resplendent airline.

When the Grand Ol' Lady takes up a westerly heading and glides through the blue horizon, she will carry a cargo of gratitude and memories placed aboard by us mortals, our everlasting thanks for the phenomenal era she willed to us. May she rest easy in that big hangar in the sky. I still think about it and it all seems like a dream, but it's a good dream, and I remember.

I Remember

I heard my dream, among the clouds.
I heard that sound like thunder loud.
The rumble of recips, like drums that roll.
Their steadfast throb, that echoed miles.

With steady cadence that stirred my soul.
With beating heart, I answered the call.
With sun, moon and stars above, I shared the sky.
Found friends who dreamed my dreams on high.

We laughed, we trusted those friends of mine.
Through time that hurried by.
Like thunder that dies, the recips have gone.
Like time that ages, I miss that gang.

Twilight is gone, yet I abide.
I remember, I listen, but all is quiet.
I hang my head, I'm all alone.
I can't look up, my dream is gone.

—Tex

The DC-3

Her nostalgic echo rings o'er the mountains
Whose summits call for a friend who is gone
She challenged and braved the windswept heights
And flirted with peaks embraced in sky

Then accosted deep canyons immersed in mist
And skipped on updrafts from a crested ridge
Stole sweeping views reserved for eagles
Enjoyed soft breezes caressing valley floors

The echo of her recips will linger forever
With the colleagues she brought together
An era of friends who'll never forget
A place in history is hers forever

—Tex

Footnotes: Works Cited

1. *The Epic of Flight—The Airline Builders.* Time-Life Books.

2. *The Epic of Flight—Flying the Mail.*

3. Ibid.

4. Ibid.

5. Glines, Carrol V. *The Saga of the Air Mail.*

6. Ibid.

7. *The Epic of Flight—Flying the Mail.*

8. *Salt Lake Tribune,* October 8, 1955

9. *Fifty Glorious Years, Story of the DC-3*, by Pearcy.

10. *The Epic of Flight—America in the Airwar.*

11. *The Epic of Flight—Flying the Mail.*

Glossary

A-Compartment (A-Comp)—DC-3s configured to carry passengers had a smaller compartment aft of the main passenger cabin, used for hauling mail and express.

Adcock Low Frequency Range Station—named after its creator, this early method of radio navigation was designed so when a pilot was on course he can hear a steady hum in the earphones from the radio range station. If the aircraft moves to the left or right of the published course, the pilot hears the Morse code for the letter N (da dit — •) or the letter A (dit da • —). When directly over the station there is a cone of silence (no audible sound) that indicates the aircraft is over the station.

Direction Finder (Radio Compass)—This antiquated method of navigating was used by early pilots who listened to the aural sounds through the headset. The pilot manually changed the direction of a loop antenna mounted on the exterior of the aircraft until the radio goes silent (aural sounds that become null). The rotating loop antenna controls the pointer needle (sometimes referred to as the radio compass) located on the instrument panel. By doing this, the pilot was able to obtain the bearing of the radio station from the aircraft. The true bearing of a plane from a station is, therefore, obtained by adding 180 degrees to the true bearing of the station from the plane, or by subtracting 180 degrees from it.

ATC (Air Traffic Control)—a method of directing air traffic by radar and/or radio communications.

ATR (Airline Transport Rating)—now designated ATP. A certificate required by all airline captains.

BT-13 (Basic Trainer)—a low cantilever wing trainer powered by a single 450-hp Pratt & Whitney Wasp Jr. A canopy enclosed a tandem two-place cockpit. Manufactured by Consolidated Vultee.

CAB (Civil Aeronautics Board)—government agency.

Coffee Grinder—a crank used by pilots to change frequencies on the old receiver sets to tune in the published frequencies of the various radio-range and broadcast stations.

CV-340 (Convair 340)—built by Convair, the spacious 44 seat airliner was powered by two eighteen cylinder, twin row radial engines manufactured by Pratt & Whitney. The engines produced a sea level rating of 2400 brake horsepower. Radar equipped and with pressurization, this was an enjoyable step for Frontier pilots.

Dead Reckoning—a calculation of an aircraft's location without the use of navigational aids. Distance is estimated at speed traveled over the surface of the earth while using compass headings.

DEW (Distant Early Warning)—a network of radar stations located in the upper polar regions for early detection of intruding missiles and aircraft.

Embedded Thunderstorms—violent storms hidden in fair weather clouds.

FAA (Federal Aviation Administration)—government agency governing civil aviation.

Flight Service Center—a government agency for weather observations and making available flight and ground information.

H-marker (radio beacon)—an early day non-directional type radio facility that tied into the ADF (Auto Direction Finder) mounted in the DC-3. It transmitted a continuous homing signal from which the pilot could determine the aircraft position in relation to the H-marker.

ILS (Instrument Landing System)—a method of radio navigation with a localizer to show path alignment and glide slope to show proper descent elevation for guiding aircraft to the runway.

Link Trainer—a ground training device used for simulating aircraft in instrument (weather) conditions, and for aerial navigation instruction. Over 5,000 WWII pilots were trained in the Link Trainer.

Missed approach—an abandonment of an approach to the runway in weather conditions that are below the prescribed minimums to make visual contact with the runway.

Morse Code—an early day method of communication by sending coded letters of the alphabet over the airways (wireless).

Me-109, Fw-190—two excellent single-engine fighters built by Messerschmitt and Focke-Wulf flown by Germany's Luftwaffe pilots.

PT-22—built by Ryan, a low wing, single-engine aircraft equipped with a single 140 or 145-hp Kinner engine. With two open cockpits in tandem it was used as a primary trainer.

Recips—referred to as gasoline-powered aircraft engines for driving a propeller.

VOR (Visual Omni Range)—send constant radio signals, or radials, in many directions like the spokes on a wagon wheel. A pilot can learn exactly where he is at all times by tuning in on the VOR stations with the Omni-Direction Finder. In bygone years it was the new method for navigating by radio for the Frontier pilots. With hi-tech navigation satellites now in the sky to display positions, the VOR is on the threshold of being phased out.

About the Author

From Captain Jack Schade, FAL retired
In August 1956 a warm and lasting friendship began for me, one
that I treasure very much to this day. My pilot logbook reads that
on the thirty-first, Tex Searle and I shared the cockpit of Frontier
Airines DC-3 No. 430. Our flight was from Salt Lake City to
Riverton, Wyoming and return serving Vernal, Utah and Rock
Springs, Wyoming. This was the beginning of may enjoyable hours of
comradeship in the air in the Grand Ol' Lady. About ten years after
my retirement at the age of sixty—through Tex's efforts—I had the
privilege of again sharing a DC-3 cockpit with him on never-to-be-
forgotten flights to Montana, Colorado, and Alaska. For this special
gift I am forever indebted to Captain Searle. He has shown his love and
respect by the innumerable hours he has spent collecting, assembling,
and working to get into print these stories of a remarkable airplane and
the people who had the privilege of sharing experiences during this
exhilarating chapter of commercial aviation. I know the readers will
wish that we could all go back in time just for a little while.

Captain W.A. McChrystal (left) and Captain Jack Schade (right), with their crew chief (center) on a Majestic Airlines DC-3 flight to Alaska together with the author. This photo was taken many years after their Frontier Airlines retirement. (Photo by Tex Searle)

Captain Tex Searle

Captain Tex Searle thought of nothing but flying from his early youth. As a young boy lying on large stacks of hay (on his father's farm in Delta, Utah), he could observe the old tri-motors and biplanes flying CAM4 (Civil Air Mail) flights between Salt Lake City and Los Angeles. At age 17 Tex was serving on an aircraft carrier in the Pacific, after the war he began flying for Frontier Airlines based in Denver, Colorado. Upon retirement from Frontier as Captain in 1985, Tex served as Director of Training and later Chief Pilot for charter and mail contractors. His first love was in flying the old DC-3s on cargo runs throughout Alaska. Besides being rated on various large aircraft, Captain Searle has flown the Learjet on charter and mail runs, has flown for the U.S. Forest Service, and owned various aircraft including the "Hog," a 600-horsepower Stearman used in mountain seeding and crop spraying.

Captain Tex Searle in the cockpit of the 600-hp Stearman sprayer called "The Hog."